SAFE
&
SANE_____

Safe
&
Sane⸻⸻⸻

The Sensible Way
to Protect Yourself,
Your Loved Ones,
Your Property and Possessions

Joseph D. McNamara,
Chief of Police
San Jose, California

GD/Perigee   A Robert Wool Book

My thanks go to Bob Wool, who conceived the idea, sold it to me, and shaped the book, and to Judy Linden, for her editorial contributions and support.

Perigee Books
are published by
The Putnam Publishing Group
200 Madison Avenue
New York, New York 10016

Designed by Lee Ann Chearneyi

Library of Congress Cataloging in Publication Data

McNamara, Joseph D.
  Safe & sane.

  "A Robert Wool book."
  1. Crime prevention—United States—Citizen
participation.   2. Criminal psychology. I. Title.
II. Title: Safe and sane.
HV7431.M4   1984   362.8′8   83-22087
ISBN 0-399-50859-7

First Perigee printing, 1984
Printed in the United States of America
  2 3 4 5 6 7 8 9

I am especially grateful to G.F.B. for his work in helping to research and write this book.

J.D.M.

To my wife Rochelle, who makes all the good things possible; to the neglected victims of crime; and to good cops everywhere—the ones who care more about protecting the innocent than building meaningless arrest statistics.

J.D.M.

CONTENTS

SAFE
&
SANE_____

1

FEARS . . .

REAL AND IMAGINED

Everyone is afraid.

Afraid for themselves, their families and loved ones, their property and possessions. We wonder: what's safe anymore? Where's a safe place to live? Half of all Americans are afraid to walk alone at night, according to one recent poll I read.

When I was a street cop starting out in New York in 1956, there were criminals and violent crimes and bad parts of every town, but except for the occasional incident, they were separate from most of our lives. Today, it seems, everybody has been the victim of a mugging or burglary, or else someone they know has experienced these crimes. As a result, many people alter their whole lifestyles. They stop going out at night, becoming prisoners of their own fears. They convert their homes into fortresses. They buy guns, which they don't know how to use. They move their homes to what they hope and pray will be crime-free communities, only to find that criminals go where the money is.

We are smothered with crime news, which may or may not be accurate, but whatever it is, those bloody images and body bags on all our nightly news programs and in the headlines and photos in our local papers, heighten our fears. One report on my desk tells us that in America today a violent crime occurs every twenty-four seconds; a crime against property takes place every three seconds.

What is not included in any of the reports or the ominous data is what I encounter day after day, a spreading feeling of helplessness: There is nothing we can do to protect ourselves and those around us, or what we own.

That is not so, and that is what this book is all about. There is plenty you can do, and in the course of this book, I hope to give you a distillation of what I've learned in twenty-seven years as a cop, to share with you solid advice and preventive measures.

My own police experience began in 1956 on a beat in New York City, where my father had been in the police department for twenty-six years, my brother for thirty-three years. I became a Captain and Deputy Inspector in the NYPD, then was Police Chief in Kansas City, Missouri, and for the last seven years, I've been Police Chief in San Jose, California.

It's a good range of experience, I think. I paid my street dues in the toughest city in America, and have had a chance to live in and be part of two other, very different communities. In a way, each has broadened my perspective, as a cop and as a man. I also had a chance to broaden myself with academic work and managed to get a doctorate from Harvard along the way.

Over the years, like other professional cops, I learned to anticipate the actions of criminals, to understand the way their minds work, to take precautions against their techniques. I want to share my experience with you because that kind of anticipation can help you to avoid dangerous situations, and permit you to take steps, sometimes simple ones, that will spare you violence, or prevent a burglar from breaking into your home.

In Chapter 2, for example, we'll consider the rapist and his psychopathic ways. I'll tell you about ten of his most common deceptions, and with each we'll see what you might do, confronted with such a situation, to escape. Some of my advice will seem fairly obvious to you, once you look at things from a different perspective, and that's fine. Common sense can save your life.

In various sections of the book, we'll consider meeting violence with violence, namely, fighting back. What can you actually do if you are confronted by a rapist with a knife in his hands, or a robber pointing a gun at you and demanding all your money? There's plenty you can do, if you use your mind and your wits, and stay cool. But there's a great deal of misinformation about disarming criminals, lashing out with surprise kicks and punches. If someone got the drop on me and pointed a gun at me, I wouldn't resist, even though I've been trained to take a gun away and, in fact, I'm pretty good at it. I would, however, start talking and be thinking several steps ahead, waiting for the chance to escape, if I could, or make a move on him, if I had to. The idea is to be safe, not even. But before physical violence is applied, there is much I could try, and so could you, as we'll see.

Defending yourself today usually raises the question of owning a gun. I am against it, with a few exceptions, and I'll make all my reasons clear. Guns are dangerous weapons to have lying about a house, especially where there are children. I've seen too many tragedies, and besides, there are so many alternatives available for protection. You'll see how various alarm systems, even barking dogs, can discourage the great majority of burglars.

Older citizens have it especially tough these days, being such easy marks for criminals. Yet, again, the patterns of these crimes show us several easy steps older persons can take for greater safety, and just as important, to dispel the fear that so enshrouds their frail lives.

We'll talk about all the things you can do, as well as what you can't do. You cannot, if you want to stay alive, try to become Superman or Wonder Woman. Life is not what you see on your favorite TV show about cops and robbers. If someone actually confronted you with a gun or a knife, only in the movies and in your fantasies would you lash out with your perfectly timed kung-fu kick, sending the weapon flying, after which your perfectly timed John Wayne right hook would flatten the mug.

Misplaced bravery, being macho instead of using your head, causes countless deaths and horrible injuries. Take, for instance, the Three-Martini Heroes, two men who were robbed at gunpoint one night after leaving a restaurant with their wives.

Two kids held them up, lifted their wallets and pocketbooks, and ran. After a moment, the two men, both middle-aged, ran after the youths. A couple of blocks later, one of the kids turned around and opened fire. He hit both men, badly wounding them. One recovered, but the other was crippled for life.

At the hospital, I said to the doctor who was treating the men, "I don't understand how they could chase after those kids. They knew they were armed. What got into them!"

"Three martinis," the doctor answered.

Using your head also means gaining perspective on the real crime conditions in your community and in your life, as opposed to what *seems* to be around you.

Not long ago in the *San Jose News*, for example, we had the headline: "Homicide No. 34—City Setting a Bloody Record," which was a statement that could understandably disturb the average reader. To a point, the facts were accurate: thirty-four people had been killed in the city that year. But if you were a citizen wondering about your safety, the numbers were not so important as the details.

The city's first homicide victim was an abandoned baby found in a dumpster. The second was a woman shot by a drunken stranger at 2 A.M. in a dreadful bar on the east side of town. Homicides numbers three and four took place at the same bar in such a bizarre double shooting that my investigators didn't know who to charge with what. These four murders had absolutely nothing to do with the average law-abiding citizen. Keep out of really bad bars like that, especially at 2 A.M., and you are far less likely to get killed. Yet by glancing at that headline you'd think San Jose had become a war zone.

Similarly, I recently discovered that downtown San Jose had what the media called "a rape wave." The mayor reacted by saying she was going to hand out free whistles to everyone. You'd think that every woman who walked the streets was going to get raped. Well, it turned out that more than half the victims were prostitutes. Of course the law doesn't permit you to rape a prostitute. Nevertheless, this circumstance alters the situation for the average woman, who is not out working the streets at night, trying to pick up strangers and exposing herself to rapists.

I don't mean to suggest that the staggering amount of crime we have in America today is not a reality, that it's the creation of newspapers and television. It is real, but it's important to perceive it in relation to your own particular life. And it's important to try and perceive it without hysteria.

Take crime statistics. I'll cite various numbers throughout this book, and they are not cheerful data. But at least they are accurate, unlike most crime figures.

The famous FBI annual crime reports, for example, are largely useless. They simply reflect conditions that police chiefs around the country choose to report, as well as the needs of local and national politicians.

Crime, of course, makes good politics. When I was a cop under Mayor Wagner in New York, crime figures always dropped when he started to campaign. This was standard operating procedure. Mayor John Lindsay amazed us all by saying he wouldn't play that numbers game—and he stuck to his word.

In Philadelphia, when Frank Rizzo was mayor, police reports showed crime going down. However, Justice Department studies found that all levels of crime actually increased, and one federal study revealed that Philadelphia had five times as many burglaries as were shown on police reports to the FBI.

It can, and often does, work the other way as well. Police chiefs give the orders, and crime statistics go up and up and up. This lets them hire more cops. When people get sufficiently scared, they are only too happy to have their city fathers increase police-department budgets. Then after a couple of years the chiefs can issue other orders, and the crime statistics go down and down and down, which, of course, conclusively proves that adding those extra cops to the force really paid off.

Hard, sensible advice and perspective are what I'm reaching for with this book, and what I also try to extend to the cops who work for me. Knowledge breeds confidence.

The good street cop approaches his work confident that he is smart enough to catch criminals. You say: He is armed, so no wonder he's confident. The fact is, no good cop relies on his gun. In all likelihood, he will go through his entire career and never fire the thing. The reasons for his confidence run much deeper than that revolver.

You are not going to become a street-smart cop from one book. But you can become a crime-smart citizen, and give yourself a safer, calmer, saner life.

2

RAPE

In the crowded parking lot of a large shopping center, Pamela Kendrick walks to her Firebird. A stranger approaches. He has been waiting for Pam to return since she pulled into the shopping center early this morning.

"Lady, I think you're leaking transmission fluid," he tells her. Pam is a bit startled by the stranger's voice. The man introduces himself as Larry, which is not his real name. He squats down in front of the car and shows Pam a puddle of oil. "I'd be awfully careful about starting up that car if I were you."

Pam stares at the spot. She knows little about cars. "Now what am I going to do?" Pam mumbles aloud to herself. She turns to Larry, who seems genuinely concerned about her car troubles. "Should I call a garage and get it towed?"

"You could," Larry tells her. "But, I don't know . . . maybe I could fix it for you. Save you some towing charges."

"Could you?" says Pam. "God, that would be very kind." Larry rolls up his sleeves and tells Pam to get inside the car and wait until he motions for her to turn the ignition key. He raises the hood, tinkers with the engine until no one is in sight, then signals for Pam to start the car. As soon as the engine turns over, Larry slams the hood, jumps into the passenger seat and pulls out a knife. "Get moving," he commands.

Pam can't believe it. She is a happily married secretary who lives in a quiet neighborhood with her husband and two children. The only criminals she'd ever encountered were on *Charlie's Angels*, her favorite television show. Ten minutes ago, Pam was fortunate to meet a man kind enough to fix her car. Now he is threatening to kill her.

Larry is an attractive man with bright blue eyes, a fair complexion, neatly trimmed mustache and broad shoulders. He speaks articulately and wears tight designer jeans. He is also an ex-convict who served seven years in the state pen for rape. As he has with other women, he has tricked Pam into becoming a prisoner in her own car.

Larry orders her to drive to a remote area, where tall weeds line both sides of a winding creek. Pam hasn't the foggiest notion where she is. She thinks about screaming but decides against it because all the windows are shut. Larry puts the knife to Pam's throat and tells her to pull over and take off her pants. She screams, but Larry puts his hand over her mouth and warns in a raspy voice, "Shut up! I don't want to kill you."

Larry rips open Pam's bra and squeezes her breasts. She lets out another yell, but no one can hear. Larry shoves Pam around so she is lying on her back and her head is resting against the passenger-side door. Her pants are down to her ankles. A couple of tears roll down Pam's cheeks, but Larry doesn't notice. He pulls her legs apart and rapes her.

Throughout the ordeal, he holds a knife near Pam's neck. When he is finished, he throws her out onto the ground and drives off.

Her clothes torn and her face bruised, Pam wanders for an hour before a passerby spots her. By the time police gather all the details, they have determined that Pam was Larry's sixth rape victim in the last month. Later, the Firebird is found. But Larry has vanished again.

Like many rapists, Larry excels at getting his victims to trust him. I call him a "Good Samaritan" rapist. By that I mean he uses one of ten common tricks—in this case the Good Samaritan routine—to capture women. I'll discuss each of these tricks in this chapter and tell women how they can protect themselves from falling into the same trap Pam did.

Pam thought she knew what a rapist looked like, and Larry did not fit the image. He was not supposed to look so trustworthy. Or handsome. As much as Pam hates to admit it, she remembers being attracted to Larry when he first offered help. She is not alone. Thousands of women make the mistake of trusting a complete stranger because his looks are appealing.

Many women think of rapists as ugly, overweight goons who stand out like a pair of white socks being worn with a three-piece suit. No description could be further from the truth. If there is such a thing as a typical rapist, he is soft-spoken, friendly and highly skilled at making women feel comfortable in his presence. Indeed, many rapists seem to be perfect gentlemen. More often than not, they are average-looking in appearance and dress. They are cautious and thorough in their planning. Sometimes they spend days searching out their victims. They use surgical gloves, baby powder, ladders, glass cutters, wire clippers, pocket knives and rental cars to accomplish their task. A rapist may be a close friend, a doctor, a repairman, a total stranger or, in rare instances, even a police officer. Recently, a California rapist was sentenced to thirty-one years in prison for sexually assaulting seventy-one women. He was a thirty-eight-year-old business executive with a $60,000 salary. So much for the goon image.

Rapists come in all shapes and sizes. They come from every race, religion and social and economic background. Men who rape often have normal relations with their wives or girlfriends. Others have trouble keeping a steady relationship. Many rapists get along well with children and are well liked by friends and associates. But these men share an intense hatred for women. For them, the joy of rape is being able to degrade and torture.

Interestingly, statistics show that many rapists were neighborhood prowlers as teenagers. They usually begin by being Peeping Toms but eventually "graduate" to rape because watching a woman through a bathroom window loses its appeal after a while. They become voyeurs for the risk, not to see a naked body. The thrill of rape comes from pulling it off against steep odds. Like the climber who conquers a dangerous mountain, a rapist assaults women for the challenge. The greater the challenge, the better. When a rapist first starts out, he is usually deterred by a barking dog. But as he becomes more experienced, the dog's presence only makes the task more risky, hence more exciting. A rapist's greatest satisfaction comes from overcoming obstacles and controlling women—not the sexual act itself. Many people mistake rape for a crime of sex. It is a crime of power. Most rapists get almost no sexual pleasure out of fondling a woman's breasts. Rather, they enjoy violating a woman's body as a further demonstration of their power. For most rapists, the real pleasure is the hunt and capture.

In strict legal terms, rape is the act of sexual intercourse against a woman's will by a man who is not her husband. (In some states, a husband can be charged with raping his wife.) Rape usually occurs under the threat of force and violence, or fear of injury and death, though juries have at times convicted doctors of raping their female patients after administering drugs. Rape also can include instances where a mentally retarded victim does not resist because she is incapable of fully understanding what is taking place.

It is not rape if the man's penis does not penetrate the woman's vagina. Anything less is defined in legal terms as sexual assault, a crime that carries lighter jail sentences in most states. But, if a man forces a woman into having oral or anal sex, that is sodomy. Under the law, sodomy is treated just as seriously as rape.

Rape is the fastest growing violent crime in this country. A rape occurs every six minutes in the United States. That's 10 rapes every hour, 240 rapes a day, 1,680 per week. And those figures only take into account the rapes reported to police. When you consider that one of every two rapes committed goes unreported, the numbers rise to more than 3,000 each week.

So much for figures. The purpose of this chapter is not to scare you with statistics. I want to alert women that they need to protect themselves against the possibility of rape. If they do, it is unlikely they will ever become victims.

In my twenty-seven years of police work I have learned that all women are not in equal danger of getting raped. It may seem obvious to you, but here are a few facts about rape that every woman should know: Nearly half of all rape attacks take place outdoors between 6 P.M. and midnight. Women who are single, divorced or separated have a greater chance of getting raped than women who are married or widowed. The same goes for women at lower income levels. (That should dispel the widely held belief that wealthy women are prime targets of rapists.) Nor is it true that women who dress in a "provocative" or "suggestive" way get raped more often than so-called "decent," "virtuous" women. Neither myth can be substantiated by police statistics. In most cases, beauty means very little. Many rapists have testified that they didn't remember what their victims looked like.

TEN COMMON TRICKS USED BY RAPISTS

All women, regardless of age, occupation or marital status, need to be concerned about rape. Here are ten common tricks used by rapists and some effective measures for women to defend themselves against them.

1. The Good Samaritan

The Good Samaritan rapist has one goal in mind—to trap a woman so that she's all alone. He doesn't confine himself to shopping-center parking lots, either. He can be found lurking around apartment buildings or waiting to help a woman carry laundry to her doorstep. Once she opens her door, bam! He forces his way inside.

The Good Samaritan's ploy also can be used inside a department store. A man taps a woman on the shoulder in a store aisle and informs her that her car has been hit in the parking lot. The woman assumes the man is a member of the shopping center's security force. How else would he know that her vehicle has been hit? She follows him back to the car, where she finds a dent in the front fender. (The rapist put it there.) In much the same way Larry trapped Pam in her Firebird, the man kidnaps the woman once she unlocks the car door.

ADVICE: Go back to the beginning of this chapter and think about how Larry was able to get Pam inside her car. He started by informing her that something was wrong with the Firebird. Pam should have realized right away that a stranger has no way of knowing a car won't run unless he tries to start the engine first. If she had trouble starting her car and then Larry offered help, that's one thing. But it is highly unlikely that a strange man is suddenly going to appear on the scene to assist you before you even get inside your car. So if a stranger informs you of car problems you are not aware of, don't believe him. Return to the store immediately and seek help from a security guard.

Women also need to be aware of the Good Samaritan trick if they are stranded alone in a car. Many women still fantasize that an ideal way to meet Mr. Wonderful is for him to fix their flat tire and then ask them out to dinner. That may work in the movies, but don't ever put yourself in such a vulnerable position. If you have car troubles and are approached by a stranger, don't get out of your car to greet him. Ask him to call a tow truck. If he insists on fixing the problem himself, be firm and tell him you want an expert. If he is sincere, he won't be offended by a woman who looks after herself. If he *is* offended, that's tough. Too many women get attacked each year because they are too polite to hurt a man's feelings.

2. The Guilt Trap

Recently, my department arrested on a rape charge a young man whose victims actually invited him into their rooms. Like many rapists, he was extremely clever. He was twenty-three, black and an ex-convict. He spent most of his time on a college campus stalking white female students. (He could have just as easily been a white man chasing black female students.) Once he picked his victim, he "accidentally" bumped into her between classes and started a friendly conversation. He then asked the student if he could borrow one of her textbooks overnight.

The normal reaction of any young woman is to resist a stranger's advance. The rapist anticipated this and pretended he was deeply hurt. He claimed the woman was uneasy because of the color of his skin. "I bet if I was white, you wouldn't turn me down." He wanted to make the coed feel that if she didn't give in to him, she was a racist. Because none of the women had ever been accused of bigotry, each felt sorry for the rapist and agreed to lend him the book for a night.

The man was not interested in reading Shakespeare or anything else. He was barely literate. He borrowed books as a way to begin the hunt. He insisted on meeting the woman again and again until he gained her trust. Eventually, she asked him to her place. Several women who fell for his act were raped under their own roofs. In court, the prosecutor was not able to convict the man because all of his victims had invited him to their rooms.

ADVICE: It's not unusual for a stranger to fall asleep in a living room after a party in a college fraternity, dormitory or apartment. College campuses are open places where young people easily meet one another. That's why rapists often work in these locations. They know that an eighteen-year-old female student is less likely to question their advances than a forty-five-year-old housewife.

If you think through the motives of a total stranger who is anxious to meet you, you won't get suckered into falling for such a scheme. As much as we need to be concerned about race relations in this country, don't forget that if a strange man, black, white or yellow, approaches, you still need to take some common-sense precautions. If he forces himself on you, don't give in just because he makes you feel uncomfortable. Follow your instincts.

3. The Disguise Artist

A rapist who knows a woman lives alone will try anything to break into her house. One way is to disguise himself as a mail carrier, paperboy or even a police officer.

I remember a rapist—we'll call him George—whose uniform fooled several women in a large apartment complex. George knew all of his victims lived alone because only one name appeared on their mailboxes. About fifteen minutes after a woman entered her apartment, George knocked on her door with a clipboard in one hand and a package under his arm. He told the woman that he wanted to leave the box for a neighbor, whom he would call by name. How did George get the neighbors' names? You guessed it—from their mailboxes.

In each case, George asked his victims for a pencil so he could leave a note with the package. Then, as these women turned their backs, he pushed his way inside and forced them to commit various sex acts.

The women all thought George was a delivery man because he wore a uniform. Many rapists dress in outfits similar to those worn by TV repairmen, meter readers and mail carriers. All operate on the assumption that women have no idea that they are rapists searching for their next victim.

Occasionally, women are tricked into believing their attacker is a police officer. This usually happens when a woman driving alone at night in a deserted area is stopped by an automobile that resembles a police squad car. The vehicle, dark in color, is equipped with magnetic blinking lights similar to those used by unmarked police vehicles. The rapist, clad in navy-blue apparel, plays the role of a patrolman by asking a woman for identification. At some point, the phony cop orders the woman out of the car, leads her to a nearby field and rapes her.

In rare instances, real police officers have abused their authority by attacking women. A California Highway Patrol officer was recently charged with raping and killing a woman near the Nevada border. After finding the victim's car pulled over on the shoulder of a rural desert highway, detectives suspected that the officer stopped the woman for a routine traffic violation and then sexually assaulted and killed her.

One of my police officers recently had sex with a young woman he arrested for drunken driving. Instead of taking her to jail, the officer drove the woman to a school playground where they had sex. When the woman later reported that she had been raped, the police officer resigned from the force. He was later convicted of a felony.

ADVICE: It often takes a tragic mistake before people learn to stop opening their doors to strangers. Protect yourself against disguised intruders by following these tips:

1. Make sure that your doors have adequate peepholes so you can identify people on your doorstep.
2. Don't open the door (even if it has a chain) for strangers.
3. Don't be fooled by a man in a uniform. If he can't slip a package under the door, tell him to leave it outside.
4. Don't hesitate to ask a repairman or a salesman for his business card. Then call his employer to verify his identity before you let him in.

This last piece of advice also applies to police officers. I realize some women may find it difficult to demand identification from a policeman, but he is the last person you should be afraid to question. After all, we are the ones who advise you not to trust strangers.

Familiarize yourself with the police uniform in your community. Before opening your door, make sure that the man is wearing the right uniform and not something that looks the same. If you're still in doubt, ask for a phone number you can call to verify the officer's identity.

If you are stopped by an officer in an unmarked car, ask for some identification. Nearly all police departments require their officers to wear nameplates and badge numbers. If the "cop" is not wearing a badge and nameplate, and it appears that he is not legitimate, drive to the nearest fire or police station.

Women who find themselves being propositioned by an officer should remember that all police departments have strict rules against cops attempting to arrange sexual favors on duty. Don't hesitate to let an officer know that you are taking down his name and badge number if he starts acting frisky. If he persists, ask him to call his supervisor.

If you have done nothing wrong and are convinced that the policeman has sexual motives, insist that he call his supervisor before you get out of the car at his request. But keep in mind that you may have to explain in court why you did not follow the officer's lawful instruction. This is not a tactic I recommend after you've run a red light, or have had too much to drink.

Remember: You have a right to complain to the police department if an officer makes any kind of sexual advance. If you hesitate to report an officer who acts out of line, some other woman may have to pay the price. Police departments can control this type of behavior only if they learn about it. In the few cases where police officers have been convicted of sex offenses, the women who came forward to complain helped build strong cases. Because of this cooperation, these officers were usually fired or forced to resign.

4. The Telephone Caller

Many rapists use guns, knives and billy clubs to subdue their victims. For others, their only weapon is the telephone. A telephone rapist searches through the listings in a city directory for a feminine first name or an initial (which often indicates a woman, probably living by herself). He calls and, if a woman answers, tells her that she has been selected at random to participate in a survey. Or that he represents a consumer group interested in learning how much the woman spends on groceries each week. Then he asks for some personal information— age, marital status, occupation and the number of persons in the household—assuring her that the responses are kept confidential. While the answers may seem harmless, they are used to help the telephone rapist size up his victim. He might tell a single woman that she is eligible to win a trip to the Bahamas if she completes the survey in person. The rapist then shows up on her doorstep. (Some women—unaware that they would soon be raped—offered these psychopaths a friendly cup of coffee.)

Other telephone rapists answer classified ads placed in newspapers. They visit a woman's home pretending to be interested in items listed for sale. If the woman lives alone, these "want-ad" rapists return to attack. Telephone rapists also pose as photographers who want to measure a woman's bustline for a photo contest. It may sound ridiculous, but this kind of thing goes on all the time. In fact, some of the most bizarre crimes involve rapists who use the telephone.

One such case took place a year ago in San Jose. A man we'll call T.R. tricked several women into having sexual intercourse with him. Once, he called a schoolteacher late at night and whispered into the phone, "My head is really messed up. Have you got anything over there to drink?"

The woman responded in a groggy voice, "Is that you, Bob?"

"Of course it is," said T.R., assuming Bob was the name of the woman's ex-husband or ex-lover. T.R. then talked to the sleepy schoolteacher for more than an hour. He even had her go into the kitchen during the conversation and pour herself a glass of wine. How she could not tell the voice was not her ex-husband's is beyond me. As they talked amicably, T.R. sensed that the teacher still had feelings for Bob. He then told her of his lifelong fantasy. "I want to watch you have sex with someone. It's really important to me."

Incredible as it may seem, T.R. talked the teacher into going along. He told her to leave the front door open so his friend could enter and have sex. He would watch and join her afterward. T.R. drove to the teacher's residence (the address was listed in the phone book), entered through the unlocked door and had sex with the woman. When "Bob" failed to show up, the teacher called her real ex-husband, who had no idea what was going on.

My department never caught T.R. We suspect he worked his

twisted magic on a dozen women, but only two others came forward. The rest were probably too embarrassed to report it.

ADVICE: You should feel free to participate in phone surveys, but do not give information such as your name, address or marital status. Some other rules to follow are:

1. If a caller asks suspicious questions, report him to the police.
2. If you feel uncomfortable with the tone of a conversation, hang up.
3. If you live alone, do not list your telephone number in city directories. If for some reason you feel you must have your number listed, at the very least don't use your address.
4. If you live alone and feel threatened by harassing phone calls, have a male acquaintance tape a message on a recorder.

5. *The Burglar/Rapist*

Rather than spend hours on the telephone, many rapists think it is easier to break into your home. But unlike burglars, rapists break in when women are home alone, or when they are gone, to wait for them to return. The burglar/rapist usually knows a good deal about his victim in advance—the time she returns from work, the door she uses to enter her home, when she goes to sleep, etc. This information helps him prepare his attack.

When I was on the New York force, we worked a prominent case. Frank the Rapist terrorized the Columbia University campus by breaking into student apartments. Even though his rapes were highly publicized and women were warned to take extra precautions, the attacks continued. I'll never forget the permanent scars Frank left on a sophomore who lived on the outskirts of the campus. She had finished studying for an exam one night and hit the sack around 1 A.M. About an hour after the lights went out, Frank scaled the fire escape and climbed into her room through an open window. He woke the young woman and raped her in bed.

The victim, a deeply religious girl, lost her virginity to Frank that night. I arrived at her apartment within minutes after she reported the rape. I asked her some questions, and she accused me of not believing her. When I asked her if she left the window ajar, she became angry. Actually, her reaction was quite normal. She thought I was blaming her for the rape attack, when I was only trying to gather information.

From interviewing this woman, it was clear the attack would haunt her for the rest of her life. She believed in not having sex before marriage, and Frank had taken that away from her. However, had the woman installed window locks, or even put some wind chimes inside her window, she might have prevented the attack. Any noise-making device you set up on windows and doors will make an intruder's task that much more difficult. Think about the little bells that alert a shopkeeper when a customer walks into his store. The same principle applies in your home.

Had three families safeguarded their houses in San Jose, they could have thwarted a seventeen-year-old burglar/rapist. The rapist—we'll call him Tom—had already spent six months in prison for sexually assaulting his next-door neighbor. This time his victims ranged from a thirteen-year-old girl to a thirty-eight-year-old divorcée. All of the assaults took place in a fashionable section of town where housing prices approached a quarter-million dollars.

The first rape took place late one evening during the Christmas holidays. Tom entered a two-story residence through an unlocked side garage door, walked into the kitchen and grabbed a steak knife. He then entered the room where the thirty-eight-year-old woman was asleep on a couch next to her ten-year-old daughter. The woman woke up when she heard her dog biting at Tom's pantleg. She called the dog off after Tom threatened to kill the pet. (The woman told police that she would have fought with Tom if her daughter had not been present.)

Tom asked the lady if anyone else was home. She said no

one. By doing so, she blew a great opportunity to confuse him. Instead, she unconsciously encouraged him to proceed. Women should use whatever means necessary to make a rapist's task more difficult. This certainly includes lying. Don't hesitate to tell him that your husband is sleeping in an upstairs bedroom. If a rapist thinks a man is home, he might not go ahead.

After threatening to kill the woman and her daughter, Tom forced the mother to disrobe at knifepoint and raped her on the floor. During the attack, Tom held the steak knife to the woman's throat, as her daughter watched in horror.

About a month later, Tom entered a residence in the same neighborhood through another unlocked sliding door. Tom had done his homework for this one. He knew that a thirteen-year-old girl came home from school every day at the same time. He confronted the girl as she changed clothes in her bedroom, put a sweat shirt over her head and warned her not to scream. He then pulled her blue jeans down, grabbed her buttocks and vagina, and rubbed his penis against her thighs. Tom told the girl not to call police or else he would come back to kill her.

Three weeks later, Tom struck again. This time he was waiting for a seventeen-year-old girl named Wendy to come home from school. As Wendy entered her bedroom, Tom pushed her onto the bed and put a pillow over her face. He unbuttoned her blouse and bra, pressed his hands to her breasts and put his finger in her rectum. When Wendy screamed in pain, Tom threatened to kill her.

Wendy tried to distract Tom by telling him she had money in her purse. She also warned him that her older sister would be home soon. By telling him this—whether or not it was true—Wendy disrupted his plan. Instead of panicking or giving in, she kept her cool. As a result of some quick thinking on Wendy's part, the rape was never completed.

Six weeks later, Tom returned to try again. He entered Wendy's house through the same unlocked window. When he knocked her to the floor this time, Wendy was prepared. She pulled out a small knife that she began carrying after the first attack. But Tom wrestled the knife away and began molesting her again.

He left several minutes later when he heard a car door slam.

As much as we wish Wendy had stuck the knife in the right place and fixed Tom for good, she is lucky to be alive. There is one rule about defending yourself against a rapist: Whenever you do fight back, make it good. Wendy was unable to use the knife against her assailant, and she was fortunate Tom didn't use the weapon on her. The one exception to this rule occurs when your life is in danger. In this case, no struggle is too extreme.

We arrested Tom after investigators matched his photo from a portfolio to a police artist's sketch based on descriptions given by his victims. While he was in police custody, Tom told us some interesting things about how he planned to rape Wendy. He said he had observed her many times and knew her daily routine. Both times he found a back gate unlocked and climbed into the house through an open window. He did not continue the assault the first time because Wendy did not want him to. Tom said he came back because Wendy had "nice lips." He was angry at himself for not carrying out his plans to rape her.

Even though Tom threatened to hurt his victims if they reported the attacks, he knew they would probably call the police. Like most rapists, Tom did not follow through on these threats. Yet such warnings often prevent women from reporting rapes.

Occasionally, a rapist will try to fulfill his threats. Last year, a twenty-three-year-old man was sentenced to twenty-four years in prison for raping a twelve-year-old girl three times. He pleaded guilty in court after admitting to being obsessed with the thought of forcing someone to have sex with him.

The rapist had threatened to kill the girl if she told police and was bitter when she testified against him in court. He felt her parents could have stopped her from taking the stand. He offered $2,000 in cash and a car to anyone who would carry out his plan, which called for a hit man to rape and torture the girl and kill her parents. The hit man was to make clear to the girl why she was going to die. Fortunately, police learned about the plan before it was executed.

Women shouldn't let a rapist's threats stop them from calling the police. I know how scary it can be for many rape victims to notify authorities after they have been threatened. But I'm not aware of a single instance in which a woman was hurt for reporting a sexual assault. Actually, you place yourself in greater danger by failing to report violent criminals, because they are then free to strike again.

The criminals who scare me are the small number of burglar/rapists who beat their victims. These animals are not satisfied with rape; they have such an intense hatred for women that a homicide is possible whenever they attack. One recent case my department investigated involved a burglar/rapist in his mid twenties who raped older women, many of them in their eighties. This guy—we'll call him Sam—broke into the homes of elderly women who lived alone. He used a flashlight to find his way around in the dark and a knife to slash telephone cords, screen doors and windows. He raped and beat six old women until they were unconscious, then took their money and valuables, including the rings off their fingers. Sam always covered his victims' faces with pillows and threatened to kill them if they so much as looked at him.

One of Sam's victims, an eighty-nine-year-old woman, was awakened one morning when she was struck on the head. The old woman tried to scream, but every time she muttered a word, Sam hit her in the face. Toward the end, he knocked her out altogether. Sam was eventually picked up by police when he tried to pawn some of his victims' jewelry to an undercover police officer. All six of Sam's victims testified against him in court. He was put away for a long, long time.

ADVICE: Protect yourself against the burglar/rapist by safeguarding your home. (See Chapter 9 on burglary.) Some other tips:

1. Remember to always lock doors and windows.
2. Have dead-bolt locks installed on all doors that lead to the outside, and put secondary locks on sliding doors and windows.

3. Think about buying a burglar alarm system. See the burglary chapter for advice on which alarm system is best for you.
4. Leave your lights on if you plan to return after dark.
5. Have your keys in hand before you reach home.
6. If you suspect someone is in your place, leave quietly and call the police from a neighbor's house.

Also, when you hear of a threat in your neighborhood, such as the Columbia rapist who attacked women on campus, take extra precautions. So many women shrug off these warnings by thinking it could never happen to them. Well, it can. So when you hear about a rape attack near your home or work, go out of your way to protect yourself. Few rapists stop after one attack. They usually rape over and over until police catch up with them.

6. The After-Hours Rapist

It is no coincidence that nearly one-half of all rapes take place between 6 P.M. and midnight. Obviously, rapists know they are less likely to be seen in the dark. They also know that fewer people are on the streets to respond to cries for help.

A favorite nighttime spot for rapists is near bars that attract single women. In San Jose, we recently nailed a guy named Anthony for three attacks, all originating in the vicinity of the same bar. The first involved a cocktail waitress. On her way home from work late one night, the woman stopped at a red light outside the bar. Anthony jumped into the waitress's car through an unlocked passenger door, put a knife to her neck, ordered her to drive to a remote location and raped her. Afterward, the waitress told us she was so terrified of Anthony she did whatever he demanded. She later picked him from a police lineup, but not before he had tried to abduct two other women outside the same bar.

A week after the first attack, Anthony went up to a woman's car, tapped on the window and said, "Excuse me, ma'am." The woman, a salesclerk in her mid twenties, rolled down her window, and Anthony forced his way into the car. Before he managed to grab her, she broke free and ran to safety.

Flustered that he had had the woman in his grasp but lost her, Anthony waited for his next victim. Less than an hour later, another young woman emerged from the bar and walked across the dimly lit parking lot. As she searched through her purse for her car keys, Anthony jumped the woman from behind. He got hold of her keys, opened the door and pushed the woman inside. But she slipped out the passenger door. Anthony was foiled again. Nevertheless, this time he ran off with the woman's purse.

Women who stay out late at night by themselves are more likely to encounter characters like Anthony. So many are unaware of the possible danger. Sometimes they walk right into a trap without realizing it.

One woman was on the way home from a date when she got into a silly argument with her boyfriend. The woman became so upset that she jumped out of the car. The man drove home in a huff; the young woman stomped into the night to sulk over her broken romance. Several minutes later, a couple of inebriated teenagers drove past her. They circled back around the block and pulled up next to her. Both of them got out of the car and approached the woman. She tried to resist their advances, but they pulled her into the car and took turns holding her down and raping her.

When police interviewed this woman, she told us the possibility of getting raped was the last thing on her mind. She was thinking about the fight with her boyfriend, not where she was headed or who she might run into. These types of cases are crossing my desk with greater frequency. Under normal circumstances, most women would never consider walking alone late at night in a strange part of town. But after they argue with a boyfriend, they don't think.

ADVICE: The best advice is don't walk alone after dark. Women who have a job or social obligation that takes them out at night by themselves should make arrangements with someone else to accompany them or take a taxi.

If you have no choice but to go out alone, stay near well-lit areas and keep away from bushes, dark buildings and entrances to garages and alleys. Be alert to what's happening around you. If you think someone is following you, turn around and look. He'll know that you won't be taken by surprise. Then, cross the street. Change your pace. Don't let your follower know where you live. If you feel you are in danger, run as fast as you can toward light and people, or scream for help.

Women who regularly go to cocktail lounges at night should keep in mind the environment in which they place themselves. If you must frequent these places, use some common sense: Avoid bars with a reputation for trouble, and bring along a friend, male or female.

If you have to walk to your car at night by yourself, ask someone to watch until you reach your car safely. And be sure to have your keys in hand.

7. The Bumper Rapist

What's your first reaction when another driver runs into your car? After shouting a few obscenities, you'd probably get out to inspect the damage and exchange your license and registration with the other driver, right? That is precisely what a bumper rapist hopes you will do.

The bumper rapist works remote areas late at night, looking for a woman who is driving alone. When he catches up with her, he intentionally rams his vehicle into hers. The rest is scripted. She gets out to inspect the damage. He pulls out a weapon and kidnaps her. It's that simple.

ADVICE: If your car is hit late at night, stay inside. To drive off and leave the scene of an accident is against the law. However, driving to the nearest police station to report the accident because you fear for your safety is not. It's a matter of judgment. Don't put yourself in a dangerous situation because of a technical violation of the law. It is hard for me to imagine any judge or jury convicting a frightened woman for being by herself and not wanting to stop on a dark street to oblige a strange man.

If your car won't run, don't roll down your window more than an inch to talk with any stranger. Ask him to call police or a repair truck.

Always keep the doors locked. This is good advice for both men and women during all hours. I'll never forget the day a drunk jumped in my car while I was on patrol in New York City. It occurred when my partner and I sneaked over to Broadway for a quick lunch. (In those days New York cops were forbidden to leave their assigned area without permission.) I sat behind the wheel finishing some paperwork while my partner ran inside a fast-food joint. When I heard his door slam, I put the car in gear and took off. I had driven a few feet before I realized my passenger was a bum. It took some quick maneuvering on my part to kick the guy out of the squad car, pick up my partner, who was waiting on the curb, and hustle back to Harlem. Actually, I was fortunate the guy was a drunk and not a nut with a gun who hated cops. I learned my lesson. I keep my car doors locked at all times.

8. The Road Rapist

Women who travel alone have become an increasingly popular target for rapists. I've seen enough cases in recent years to convince me that female travelers need to take extra precautions on the road. Many of the cases run along these lines:

A man seats himself next to a woman on an airplane and starts a friendly conversation. When they arrive at the airport, he offers to carry her luggage or share a cab to the hotel. He has learned from their conversation aboard the plane that she is spending the night alone. At the hotel, he waits for the woman to return from dinner. When she opens the door, he forces his way into her room and rapes her. Before leaving, he yanks the telephone from the wall.

In all large cities, there are a host of rapists who work airports, bus terminals and cocktail lounges in search of women traveling alone. When a rapist offers to buy a woman a drink, he wants to learn where she is staying, how long she will be in town, who is picking her up at the airport, etc.—all information to help him plan his attack.

ADVICE: This is a difficult one for me. I don't want to make women who travel feel they need bodyguards. On the other hand, they ought to be aware of what can happen to them. You don't assume that every man who sits next to you on an airplane is scheming to get you alone in a hotel room. Most male passengers are content to chat and go their way. However, some men do follow up personal conversations by trailing women back to their hotels. So if you travel alone, keep it in the back of your mind that such characters exist.

How can you tell the difference between the man who engages in friendly chitchat and the one who is plotting a sexual attack? You can't. Police officers wish they could instantly recognize bank robbers in advance. You have to fall back on the advice offered earlier in this chapter—don't be lulled into a false sense of security because a man doesn't fit your stereotype of a rapist. Follow your instincts. If a man starts a conversation that makes you feel uncomfortable, tell him that you want to read a book. Or talk to him about how anxious you are to meet your husband and kids at the airport. You can also excuse yourself and grab another empty seat on the plane. Whatever you do, don't feel you have to be polite. If the man persists, notify an airline stewardess. They get harassed by obnoxious male passengers all the time and will be sympathetic to your complaint.

9. The Run and Hit Rapist

Female joggers, particularly those who run alone at night, are a rapist's easiest prey. Too often, they set their own trap by running after dark without a companion and in out-of-the-way areas where yelling and screaming attracts little attention. These women also run the risk of being confronted by a carload of young men who as individuals would probably never rape but as a group, attack in "gang-bang" style.

One night several years ago, a young San Jose woman had trouble sleeping. After tossing and turning in bed for three hours, she went jogging in a secluded brook area. She had gone on these nocturnal runs for years, but this time a car full of young men happened to drive by. They followed her for about a mile before they pulled her into the car and raped her in the backseat. The young lady told us later that she never realized she was putting herself in danger. She had jogged at night for years and had never come close to feeling threatened.

Probably the most frustrating statement I hear over and over from victims is "I've been doing it for years and nothing has ever happened to me." You can't imagine the number of violent crimes that police investigate each year because the victims failed to use common sense.

ADVICE: I don't want to give the impression that women who jog alone at night are asking for trouble, but they sure aren't using wise judgment. I have two teenage daughters who enjoy running in a nearby park. I don't let them jog at night unless I'm with them.

If you run alone when it's dark, stop. Don't think you are safe because you haven't been attacked yet. The odds will some-day catch up with you. I recommend that you run with a partner and, if possible, during daylight hours. Don't always run the same path, especially if it takes you through remote parks or isolated areas. And stay alert. It might seem obvious that something is wrong when a male jogger shows up on a park trail dressed in blue jeans and Western boots. But we have had two recent cases where such men have been successful in raping women runners. It never occurred to them that the unusual attire meant something was not right.

10. The Dance-Floor Rapist

A man asks a woman for a dance in a local tavern. After a few whirls on the dance floor, he escorts the woman back to her table and buys her a glass of wine. Several dances and drinks later, the man asks the woman if he can take her home.

Sounds innocent enough, right? Cocktail lounges have always been a popular place for men and women to meet. Every night, that scenario is played out in small and large cities across America. Now add the sequel from a recent southern California case: On their way out of the bar, the man tells the woman he has to stop by his apartment to check his phone messages. She accompanies him inside. Once they are in the apartment, he grabs her by the throat, punches her in the face, rips off her dress and rapes her. When she passes out, he throws her nude body into the trunk of his car and drives to a wooded area. He stabs her twenty times and buries her in a shallow grave.

Many women who frequent bars accept dates with men on the first night, thinking the evening could be the start of something big. Instead, it turns out to be the worst one-night stand possible—they are beaten, raped and robbed. In this case, the woman was later discovered by a security guard. Miraculously, the dirt and leaves that covered her body kept her from bleeding to death. Her attacker was later arrested and sent to prison for twenty-seven years. He was thirty-eight and had come to California from the Midwest, where he killed his wife three years earlier.

Another tragic case involved an independent twenty-one-year-old woman who accepted a co-worker's offer to spend a day shopping for a car. The woman did not know the man very well, but he seemed soft-spoken and polite. He was fifty-one, balding and heavyset. The woman was cautious enough to warn her roommate to notify someone if she didn't return by early evening. Three weeks later, the woman's body was found, a gunshot wound in the head, along a little-used hiking trail. She became the seventh victim whose corpse was recovered by police in mountainous areas in northern California. The man she went out with was dubbed "the trailside killer." He was an ex-convict who had spent eighteen of his last twenty-one years in prison for various sex offenses. Although the woman sensed some level of danger, she fell back on the argument—fatal, in this case—that it couldn't happen to her. Like so many other victims, she was willing to risk forming a friendship with a not-so-handsome but interesting stranger.

ADVICE: Again, this is a toughie because, as we all know, so many people do meet in bars, dance, drink, and nothing terrible happens. Yet, there are a few precautions a woman can take.

First, learn something about this stranger before you let him take you home, something about his background, where he lives, what he does for a living, who his friends are, etc.

There is nothing against the law in having a few drinks and meeting men in a bar. But play the game on your terms, not his. If you meet a guy who interests you, tell him you'd like to have dinner sometime and ask for his phone number. Or give him yours. Then arrange your first date where there will be crowds of people, at restaurants, athletic events, movie theaters, shopping centers, etc.

A woman who willingly places herself alone with a man in an environment where she is isolated from help had better know who she is dealing with. Once you get to know a person, you can take it from there, feeling comfortable that you have at least checked him out, rather than feeling used after a one-night stand. This way, you might feel better about yourself and your new relationship.

By pointing out the dangers in dating strange men, I don't mean to cramp anyone's lifestyle. After all, when I first met my wife twenty years ago on a Long Island beach, she did not know me from Joe Friday. Our first date didn't start until after I got off my midnight shift. So, I'm not telling women to stay home at night and avoid men. I am saying you should be aware there is a risk involved in socializing with strangers. You can minimize that risk by exercising a little caution.

Here's a summary of safety tips:

1. Single women living alone should put their initials on mailboxes, not their first names. Also, adding another last name gives strangers the impression that other people live there.
2. Screen all service and sales workers. Keep them outside while you call their employers to verify their identity.
3. Have your keys in hand before you reach the front door. Leave spare keys with a friend, not under a doormat.
4. If you suspect someone is in your house or apartment, leave quietly and call the police from a neighbor's place. Do not worry about imposing.
5. If you must walk alone after dark, walk briskly. Stay in well-lighted areas away from bushes, overgrown shrubbery, and entrances to garages and alleys.
6. If you are followed, go to an open business, police or fire station for help. Do not go home. Don't let your follower know where you live.
7. Jog with a friend, and vary your time and route. Avoid isolated areas, and be aware of people and places around you.
8. Keep car doors locked and windows rolled up.
9. Check the interior before entering your car, to make sure an unexpected passenger isn't hiding inside.
10. Should you encounter car trouble, raise the hood and wait inside the car for help. Lock the doors and keep them locked. Roll your window down only about half an inch, and ask anyone who stops to phone the police or a repair truck for you.

IF HE ATTACKS

By following the advice given up to now, you can protect your-self from the possibility of rape. But you also need to think about how to react in the event of a sexual attack. The issue of women defending themselves against rapists has been debated for dozens of years. At one time, police departments recom-mended that women fight male attackers to the very end. Such advice reflected society's view of rape—it was regarded as a fate worse than death. In some states, rapists got the death penalty.

Back then, police officials caught a lot of flak for telling women to put up a struggle regardless of the circumstances. Critics contended that victims who fought off armed attackers were more likely to wind up severely beaten or killed. They had a strong argument. By advising women to always use physical force against a rapist, police departments were partly respon-sible for the unnecessary knife wounds and broken bones many victims suffered.

So police switched to the other extreme by encouraging women to resist only if their lives were at stake. This new advice was equally inappropriate. Police studies showed that women who put up a struggle were often successful at preventing a rape attack. By encouraging women not to resist unless they were in a life-threatening situation, police officials were partly to blame for nationwide increases in rape.

Today, most police departments offer women more sensible advice. We recommend that women use certain defenses in certain situations; they should try to calculate the danger they are in and look for ways to escape. Often, they have a good chance of getting away.

Some feminists still suggest that women are better off fighting than submitting to a rapist under any circumstance. Such advice sounds good, but as a police officer I know all too well that women get killed for putting up too much resistance. My feeling is that a woman's best defense is to use a three-step ap-proach that starts with basic precautions. If you use physical force at the onset and it doesn't work, you may run out of options.

The first step—the use of deception—is the least dangerous level of resistance. The second step involves trying to escape without the use of force. The third step—physically harming your attacker—is a last resort.

Step 1: Working on a Rapist's Mind

Many women have avoided rape by relying on the subtle yet effective strategy of outsmarting their attacker. For these women, all it took was a little imagination. Many talked their way out by pleading. Others acted crazy, deliberately fainted, wept, vomited or pretended they were sick. Some even cooperated with their attackers by offering them a stiff drink first, then fleeing out the door. One woman asked a rapist for a date when she was being held down. He let go and was later arrested when she showed up the next day with police.

The way you talk a rapist out of attacking is to establish contact with him. Make him think of you as a human being with emotions, not as an object to be manhandled. In most cases, a rapist regards a woman as a thing to be dominated and manipulated. You can try to change his thinking by telling him he looks like your brother. Mention your children. Or ask him something personal about his family. The more he responds to your questions, the better. Keep thinking of ways to trick him. If you're inside your home, for instance, tell the rapist that your husband is upstairs sleeping. Or that your boyfriend is expected any minute.

If the rapist has a weapon, ask him to put it down. Tell him that you won't enjoy this with a gun to your head and assure him that you won't try anything sneaky. Think ahead and plan an escape so that if the rapist puts the weapon down, you can get away.

There are also a couple of things you should never say to a rapist. Never tell him that you know him or that he won't get away with attacking you. By doing so, you are only reminding him to cover for his crime by leaving a body—instead of a witness—behind. For the same reasons, you don't want to make it obvious that you are studying his face so that you can identify him later.

Step 2: Leaving the Rapist Behind

The object here is to escape by attracting the attention of others, or running away. These are feasible options only when people are nearby. So try not to let the attacker take you to a deserted area. Since women who let out a loud scream run the risk of getting punched in the mouth, don't yell unless you suspect someone is nearby.

A good device that will attract attention is a shriek alarm. The size of a lipstick tube, a shriek alarm lets out a penetrating blast that can be heard for great distances. It sells for about $5 and ties around your wrist. It has a distinct sound and is activated by the push of a button. A rape whistle is another noisemaker worth considering.

A surprising number of women have escaped without using force by keeping their cool and anticipating an opportunity to run away. If a rapist is driving toward a remote location, think about jumping out when the car is stopped at a red light. Or consider fleeing when the rapist pulls his pants down. Before he can chase you, he has to get dressed again.

Step 3: Fighting Your Way Out

If all else fails, then it is time for you to consider using force. Remember that your first priority is to get away. If you choose to get physical, make sure it works. If it doesn't, you may wind up getting seriously injured or killed.

For some women, defending themselves against a rapist means running and screaming, no more. Others have taken self-defense courses and are well trained in the use of firearms. Wherever you stand, don't attempt to use physical force if you have any hesitancy about hurting someone. This may sound strange, but many women do not battle it out with rapists. The best police statistics indicate that about half of all rape victims do not resist. You may ask how could any woman possibly not put up a struggle with a man who is about to violate her body. Well, when a strange man threatens to kill you, you're more likely to follow his orders. The natural human reaction of a woman who is confronted by a rapist and is not familiar with the kind of advice we're considering is to panic or to freeze. The average woman hasn't thought about how she could react if she were attacked. She thinks it can't happen to her. This is why I have taken you through a number of actual rapes—so you can toss the cases around in your mind and have some understanding of the dangers you face and how you can overcome them.

I think I have described enough about the violent nature of rapists to convince women that they are justified both morally and legally in using whatever force is necessary. This includes biting a rapist's hand, poking a finger in his eye or kicking him in the groin. No matter how large or powerful a man might be, his eyes, genitals, windpipe and shins are all susceptible to a swift blow. Contrary to popular opinion, kicking him in the balls is not the best course of action. Officers are taught in police academies that the best place to inflict pain is in the shin or kneecap areas. If you aim for a rapist's groin and miss, you'll probably hit him in the stomach or thigh, where it doesn't hurt so much.

Another possibility is to grab a sharp object, such as a steel comb, from your purse. Since you want to disable your attacker, don't try to get cute. If you slash him in the face and he recovers, you could pay for the mistake with your life. Take what openings you have and use the sharp object to poke him in the eye. If you have a knife, stab him in the lower chest or stomach area. You want to nail him in a fleshy area where the knife will penetrate, not a bony area like the shoulders or arms.

Mace is another weapon many women should consider. It is small enough to carry in your pocket yet potent enough to quickly disable. Of all the weapons a woman can arm herself with, I recommend Mace. It is the one overpowering tool that can be pulled out in an instant. Before carrying Mace in many states, you must complete a training course and obtain a permit. To use Mace, you depress the button on the top of the tube and shoot a stream into the rapist's face. Obviously it would be better to let him have it between the eyes, just as it helps to shoot a man through the heart. However, you are better off aiming at a wide target. If you hit someone in the facial area, you've got him. Then, get the hell out of there. Don't threaten a rapist with Mace as if you were waving a handgun. The element of surprise is one of the reasons I recommend Mace. Just make sure you squirt your attacker before he can recover and defend himself.

I can't give you a list of rules that will work in every rape case—there is no single or simple plan to thwart a sexual attack. You've got to use common sense. A woman must assess the situation and make her own choices. In general, if your attacker threatens to kill you and you have reason to believe him, then you should put up the strongest resistance possible. If you think you can prevent a rape from occurring by using some form of self-defense, go ahead. But if you feel you are trapped in a corner, wait for a better opportunity to come along. The woman who keeps her cool usually comes out unharmed.

AFTER AN ATTACK

Should your attempts fail, don't give up. You'll want to take mental snapshots of the attacker so that you can help police find him later. Remember his height and weight, the color of his skin, hair and eyes, his clothing, his car, license number (if at all possible) and anything unusual. The information is vital to convict rapists and put them behind bars.

Immediately after an attack, all rape victims should take the following steps:

1. Go to a safe place. If you are in a deserted area, toward
    people and lights. If at home, call a friend or go to a
    neighbor's house.
2. Preserve evidence. Blood, semen and pubic hair are im-
    portant evidence that can be used in court. Don't shower
    or douche, change your clothes, or disturb the crime scene.
3. Call police. An officer will respond quickly if you report
    the attack right away. He will ask you for a description
    of your attacker and take you to a medical facility.
4. Get medical care. Many rape victims have injuries they
    are not aware of; a rape crisis volunteer will help you
    with pregnancy prevention and venereal disease treat-
    ment, and anything else you might need.

Many of us consider it our civic duty to report serious crimes
such as rape, but about half of all rape victims do not call police.
Some are too embarrassed. Many feel guilty that they didn't
fight off their attacker. Others are afraid that their husbands,
boyfriends or relatives will find out. Also, rape victims fear
retaliation, newspaper publicity, having to recount the crime
for police and facing their attacker in court.

Much of the blame for this reluctance to report rapes rests
with the police. For years, we gave rape victims very little
sympathy. More often, rape was regarded as a big joke. I remember the New York police sergeant who discussed rape in
my first training class. "Today, men, we're going to talk about
assault with a friendly weapon," he said. Everyone laughed.

Happily this cynicism toward rape victims no longer exists
in most police departments. The good ones now have sexual
assault investigation units with officers on call twenty-four hours
a day. These officers—both male and female—are specially trained
to treat rape victims with dignity and to be sensitive to their
needs. A rape investigator's job is to help guide rape victims
through the investigative process, as well as to gather evidence
against their attackers.

If your police department does not have a sexual assault

investigative unit, then you are missing a very important service. You have the right to demand an explanation from your police chief and your mayor.

Despite improvements in handling rape investigations, many women continue to keep rape a secret. In some cases, you can hardly blame them. Although public pressure has changed courtroom procedures so that rape victims are no longer harassed on the witness stand, women still feel the law works against them.

Take the case of a University of San Francisco student who reported to campus police that she had been raped by Quintin Dailey, the star player of the school's basketball team. The campus public safety officers in her case ignored standard police procedure in a rape investigation. They did not collect any physical evidence from the victim; they took no fingerprints; they did not take the victim to a hospital for a medical examination; and they did not report the attack to San Francisco police. It wasn't until several days later, when the student decided to go to the police herself, that Dailey was charged with rape. By then it was too late to collect any evidence that might have helped convict Dailey. While the university was lax in its efforts to assist the victim, it did help Dailey choose a high-priced attorney.

The woman, a senior honors student involved in numerous church and campus programs for the poor, believed a campus public safety department officer had tried to discourage her from reporting the attack. He cautioned her against pressing charges, and warned her of the tremendous publicity she would face if she accused a star athlete like Dailey of rape. When the woman did report Dailey to police and the story made headlines, sportswriters for San Francisco's two major newspapers wrote stories that intimated Dailey was probably innocent. The only public expression of support in the victim's behalf came from a San Francisco rape crisis group that criticized the newspapers for showing more concern for the reputation of the school's basketball team than about violence against women. In the end, Dailey pleaded guilty to one count of aggravated assault in exchange for a promise that he would not go to jail for raping the woman.

THE TOUGH BUSINESS OF REPORTING THE FACTS

Women who do report rapes to police often find it hard to recount the details. Many are interviewed only hours after the attack and are still in a state of shock. These women, their friends and relatives often grow furious over police questioning. They do not understand that a police investigator must ask some very direct questions. Otherwise, he risks having a rape conviction overturned if he helps a victim describe the attack. Take the following interview between a sexual assault investigative officer and a rape victim.

Investigator: "Tell me what happened."
Victim: "He raped me."
Investigator: "What do you mean by rape?"
Victim: "He stuck his thing into me."
Investigator: "Which thing are you talking about?"

The victim is livid. She has been raped and has dragged herself to the police station. Now she is being ridiculed by an "insensitive" police officer. But look at it from the officer's viewpoint. He has to be absolutely certain that when the victim says the rapist stuck his "thing" into her, she is talking about his penis and not his finger. Many women are embarrassed to describe to a police officer how they were raped. Let's pick up with the interview.

Victim: "He put his penis into me."
Investigator: "Where?"
Victim: "Where do you think?"
Investigator: "I need to know where."
Victim: "My vagina."
Investigator: "Did he have an erection?"
Victim: "I think so."
Investigator: "Did he take your clothes off?"

> Victim: "No."
> Investigator: "How did he rape you?"
> Victim: "He made me unzip my pants."
> Investigator: "Did he have a weapon?"
> Victim: "He had a knife."
> Investigator: "Where was the knife during the rape?"
> Victim: "I think he was holding it in his hand."

The interview can go on like this for some time. The above conversation is not real, and indeed many police interviews of rape victims are not held on a strict question-and-answer basis. The detective usually tries to coax the information out of a rape victim during an informal conversation. Nevertheless, you can imagine how disturbing such a session can be for a victim.

All of these details are necessary for an officer to conduct his investigation. He needs to know where the rapist put his penis because it is a different crime depending on the part of the body that was violated. He needs to know if penetration was made because of the legal difference between rape and sexual assault. It also is important for the investigator to determine whether or not the sex acts were forced so he can determine the strength of the case. Remember, if you don't report your assault immediately, your case will be difficult to prosecute. Even if you wait, though, you should still give police information that might prevent future assaults by the same rapist.

A rapist is caught and convicted only with the victim's assistance. Her description of both the events and the person who attacked her is crucial to any investigation. The victim usually doesn't realize that she is probably only one of a number of women who have been attacked by the same person. When the police hear a description of the rapist and details of the attack, they are often able to use this information to capture ex-convicts who have committed similar types of crimes in the past.

Rape is a difficult crime to prove in court. I'd like to have a nickel for every time a rape took place and the jury did not convict the suspect. In these cases, the major stumbling block to getting a conviction is proving that the woman did not consent to intercourse.

One case in Harlem involved a woman who reported that a gunman raped her four times. She told us she was convinced he would have used the gun if she hadn't given in. When we asked her why she was so sure, she told us he was a violent person. She had dated this guy before and had had sex with him a number of times. Now this doesn't mean that the guy didn't rape her. But we knew we had our work cut out for us. During the twenty-four hours she was held captive, the rapist had taken her with him when he went to get a haircut. He double-parked his car and left her alone in the front seat while he went into the barbershop. The woman told us she didn't leave the car because the man still had the gun. She believed that if she had left, the man would have gotten up from the barber's chair and shot her.

The case was dismissed in court. The judge decided that the woman was a voluntary participant in sex because she had ample opportunity to escape and did not. While this case may sound a bit outrageous, such incidents are all too common.

Another New York case during my patrol days involved a young woman who told police that she was accosted in front of her apartment, taken to the 15th floor and raped. The woman appeared very calm as she spoke to police. Again, this means very little. Investigators are taught not to draw any conclusions about the credibility of a victim's story based on her behavior.

When we asked her to describe the assailant, the woman said he was about twenty-one or so, and very good-looking. Right away our ears perked up. The normal reaction of a rape victim is to display hostility toward her attacker. But just because she described him as very handsome did not mean the rape did not occur. As the interview progressed, she told us that the rapist was nervous and inexperienced. "He didn't seem to know what he was doing," she said. "At one point, I had to get on top of him."

We asked about the knife. She said she wasn't sure, but the weapon was probably underneath him. We knew that no judge in the land would rule that this woman was forced to have intercourse with the rapist when she admitted getting on top of him.

Both cases illustrate how the real world differs from the legal world. The first woman thought her attacker would leave the barber's chair and shoot her. The second felt she had to help the rapist, or he would use the knife on her. But because it was clear the one woman had had an opportunity to escape and the other had voluntarily changed positions, the legal element of rape simply did not exist.

A recent California case shows yet another way that rapists avoid prosecution. It involved a woman who had accepted some cocaine from a friend at a party and then accompanied the guy to his room. The suspect punched her in the face, choked her and then raped her. When he finished, the suspect fell asleep and the woman fled. In court, the woman admitted that she had accepted some cocaine from the suspect and that she had voluntarily accompanied him upstairs. But she testified that she did not intend to have sex with him and had vigorously resisted his advances. The defense attorney told the jury that group sex is common at parties where drugs are offered to guests. He described how none of the partygoers in that setting were surprised to learn the two had had sex. In fact, the attorney said, the partygoers probably would have thought it unusual if they hadn't.

The jury bought the argument, and the suspect was acquitted. Had the victim known that rape convictions are rare when a woman accompanies a man to his room, she might have thought twice about going upstairs with him. Don't put yourself in such a vulnerable position. If you do, you'll get little sympathy from a panel of jurors. And your attacker will be back on the streets to start all over again.

Sadly, it is often easier for a rapist to sexually assault a woman than it is to convict him of the crime. Many cases are dismissed because they don't stand up in court.

Cops are frustrated by this every day, but that's the way it is. Some rapists are caught. Others get away. I don't want to discourage any woman reading this book from reporting serious crimes. Without victims to assist police, rapists will walk free.

By reporting a rape, a woman becomes eligible for a number of services, including police protection, free hospital care, assistance from women's support groups and possible monetary benefits from a victim's rights program. More important, if you don't report rape, your ordeal becomes a secret, which may lead to psychological problems on your part. Rape is not a crime any woman should feel ashamed of. She should feel outraged and demand that justice be served against her attacker. And by facing up to the attack instead of hiding from it, you will help yourself recover from its trauma.

3
GUNS

Stashed under the counter of Margaret Stinson's family-owned liquor store in suburban Detroit were two handguns. Margaret had hoped she'd never have to use the things. She hated them. But after the store was robbed two years ago, she enrolled in a weapons class at the local firing range. She wanted to be able to protect herself just in case her store was ever robbed again.

Last year it happened. Two gunmen wearing ski masks held up the store. One put a pistol to the head of Margaret's teenage son and the other demanded money. As she began emptying the cash register, Margaret tripped the silent alarm. Her husband rushed out of his office and was shot in the left side. Margaret calmly reached under the counter for the .357-caliber magnum handgun and the other gun, and the forty-four-year-old mother started blasting away, a gun in each hand. Bystanders hit the floor and bullets peppered the newspaper stand. When it was over, Margaret had killed both robbers. One was hit by five bullets. The other got it three times.

The people in the Michigan town were so impressed with Margaret's marksmanship, they would have elected her sheriff. To them, Margaret's heroics proved that the little man, or woman, could triumph over the feared criminal.

Stories like Margaret's are recounted everywhere by gun lobbyists who believe that unarmed, law-abiding citizens are at the mercy of violent criminals. One such group, the Citizens' Committee for the Right to Keep and Bear Arms, recently ran an advertisement that showed the muzzle of a handgun pointed at a shopkeeper. It read: "Last week, the government came and took this shopkeeper's gun away." It continued: "When honest people give up their guns, the criminals among us aren't going to. So with gun control, only the thieves, thugs and insane killers will have guns. And that's a real danger. To our country and to you."

The ad relies on fear to persuade ordinary people that without guns they're in deep trouble. Don't be deceived by these scare tactics. Most police officials like myself will tell you that people like Margaret are fortunate to be alive. The sheriff in Margaret's hometown refrained from getting caught up in the hoopla that followed the shootings. Nor did he encourage other merchants to stock their shelves with handguns. He knew that tragedies frequently happen when ordinary folks start packing pistols.

If Margaret continues to battle it out with robbers, it'll be her corpse the coroner hauls off to the morgue. The numbers show that store owners with handguns get killed just as often as robbers. In 1979, for instance, twenty-five people were killed in New York City in shoot-outs between store owners and robbers. Thirteen were storekeepers. Twelve were crooks. If you own a handgun, these figures should tell you something.

I learned from my patrol days in Harlem that when a store owner keeps a gun, his wife stands a decent chance of collecting on his life insurance policy. I remember one grocer—we nicknamed him "Wild West"—who kept several pistols in his store. He even killed two robbers in separate holdups. On a third robbery attempt, it was Wild West who got splattered all over the tuna cases. I knew he was going to get it sooner or later. He had to. Every time he shot it out with a robber, the odds mounted against him. And he only had to lose once.

Wild West was not your run-of-the-mill handgun owner. He knew how to fire a weapon. But when the crucial moment came for him to shoot, the robber beat him to the punch. The death of Wild West convinced me long ago that the risk of owning a gun far outweighs the protection. Most law-abiding citizens who own guns will hesitate to pull the trigger; the armed robber will not. Once he reaches the stage where he points a loaded revolver in a shopkeeper's face, he has become a hardened criminal. That means he has probably committed other acts of violence. Many violent criminals consider it no big deal to take the life of a victim who resists. They've done it before and they may have to do it again. It's part of the job. You and I generally don't think that way.

Compare the robber's motivation to that of the store owner who pulls his gun and yells for the robber to freeze. Chances are the shopkeeper has never shot anyone, nor does he want to kill another human being. All he wants is for the robber to leave him alone. The person who has second thoughts about taking another life had better not wave his gun at anyone. A shred of hesitation and he can be dead.

Having a gun around is a risky proposition. Too many things can go wrong. In New York, the owner of a Chinese restaurant shot at a robber and accidentally killed his own teenage daughter. During a holdup in Nashville, a liquor-store owner ran out the front door with a gun in his hand. A young policewoman mistook him for the robber and nailed him flat on the pavement. He died.

Many merchants don't think about getting a gun until their store has been robbed. But there are other more sensible crime-prevention methods. Buying an alarm system is one. Others include keeping smaller amounts of cash on hand, increasing insurance coverage, installing video cameras, clearing windows of merchandise and hiring a security guard. These measures prevent robberies. A gun in the drawer only complicates them.

My experience as a street cop suggests that most merchants should not have guns. But I feel even stronger about the average person having them. Shopkeepers have a number of security concerns that you and I do not. They keep large amounts of cash on hand and their doors are left open to complete strangers. Most homeowners, on the other hand, simply have no need to own guns.

Further, most people don't know how to shoot a gun. They think they know. They watch TV and see Clint Eastwood or one of Charlie's Angels fire away, but that's not how it's done.

First, you try to take cover. Then you support the gun with

both hands and slowly squeeze off the bullet. The correct method of shooting a gun is similar to the way a professional photographer takes a photograph. He learns to control his breathing while slowly pushing the shutter release. Misfiring a gun is as easy as taking bad pictures. If you own a gun and are not adequately trained to use it, you could pay with your life.

Of course, you'd never know this fact from watching television. In 1977, a gun was used on TV every nine minutes during prime-time viewing hours. So it's easy to forget that once the average person pulls the trigger, everything is real: the blood, the agony, the pain and the death. Also, the weekly program never deals with how people get guns. Everyone simply has them—the lady detective, the pimp, the private eye, the bus driver. Believe it or not, most people don't have guns. So don't be misled into thinking everyone owns one.

Let's consider the dangers involved in having a firearm.

DO YOU REALLY NEED A GUN?

You've been a bit edgy for the last month since your neighbor's place was hit by burglars. You're afraid you'll be left empty-handed when your turn comes, so you purchase a weapon—your very own security blanket—something to make you feel safe at night. This sounds like it's worth rushing to the sporting-goods store, right? The gun lobby thinks so. It has manufactured all kinds of slogans: "Only the fittest survive, so if you don't want to get wasted by some thug, get yourself a gun." Or, "No burglar will dare intrude on your property if you have a gun. If he does, it'll be his hide, not yours."

Tough talk aside, none of those phony excuses warrant the purchase of a gun, particularly the stuff about protecting yourself against burglars. I know that the fear of someone breaking into your residence seems like a strong argument for getting a gun. But a burglar is in business to steal property, not to hurt people. No house thief in his right mind wants to break in when someone is home. He'd rather steal your gun in the daytime while you're at work. Guns are considered "hot" merchandise because they're so easy to sell. That's why 100,000 guns in this country are stolen each year.

For the sake of argument, let's assume you're home in bed when a burglar breaks in. You have locked up your gun to prevent your children from accidentally shooting themselves. So, unless you plan on politely asking the intruder for ten minutes to get your act together, he's going to beat you to the trigger. Similarly, a gun is not the answer to defending yourself against murder, robbery or rape because such violent crimes happen quickly, without warning to accommodate a gun owner.

In most cases a weapon won't do you any good. But it can cause you a whole lot of harm. A recent study by the U.S. Conference of Mayors found that a handgun kept in a house is far more likely to cause serious injury or death to a family member than to an intruder.

WHAT IF YOU CAN'T BRING YOURSELF TO SHOOT?

Few people realize just how difficult it is to shoot a gun. Having the power to kill someone is not something to take lightly. When they're put in such a situation, many gun owners hesitate or freeze. Some pay for such common reactions with their own lives. I know many cops surely have.

For the most part, gun owners don't think about shooting someone. They just assume that when they point a gun at someone, the person will do whatever they say. Did you ever notice how many Hollywood crooks look down the barrel of a gun? And whenever Kojak orders them to freeze, they immediately put their hands in the air. Nothing could be further from the real world. When I gave such commands to people on the street, the response often was "Fuck you, pig!" Then what do you do? Shoot someone for swearing at you?

In my twenty-seven years in police work, I have never shot at anyone. That is not to say I didn't have the opportunity.

Once, in New York, I couldn't force myself to shoot a man who came at me with a knife. My partner and I responded to a family disturbance at a run-down Harlem apartment house, where the woman inside refused to let us in. She was afraid her husband would return and kill us all. We calmed her down and told her to call if her husband showed up. Suddenly, we heard some loud noises. It was her husband stomping up the stairway. He had a large butcher's knife in one hand and a hammer in the other.

"Hold it right there. Police officers," I yelled at the top of my lungs. He kept coming toward me. "Hold it! Police!" I yelled again. He kept coming until he had me backed up against a wall. He was so close that even if I shot him, he could have leaned forward and plunged the knife into my stomach. I finally yelled, "If you move, I'll blow your head off." That must have penetrated his senses because he threw down his weapons. I would have been completely justified in killing the man, but I couldn't force myself to pull the trigger. I'm not quite sure why. Perhaps I never felt I was in real danger, though I was. And I was lucky to escape. In the end, it was fortunate I didn't shoot. The husband was never arrested, because his wife refused to press charges against him.

If a gun in the hand of a trained cop is not a sure thing, then surely a weapon in your possession isn't either. I think it's far better not to have a weapon at all than to have one and find you are incapable of using it. Unless you are a serviceman, a law-enforcement officer or some other type of individual trained to function in an emergency, you shouldn't have a gun. It could get you killed.

GETTING SHOT WITH YOUR OWN GUN

If few gun owners have thought of actually shooting someone, even fewer have considered the very real possibility of getting shot with their own guns. It may sound crazy but it happens all the time. In Kansas City, one of my patrolmen was shot and killed with his own gun when he responded to a robbery in progress at a small drugstore. The officer went into the stock area, where three robbers jumped him and took his weapon. The cop fought courageously to his death. He was twenty-three.

Each year, roughly 15 percent of police officers killed in the line of duty are shot with their own guns. That statistic should tell you something. Just as a police officer can't walk into a store and start firing at anyone who doesn't obey his commands, a gun owner must be equally cautious. You can't shoot and ask questions later. You have to assess the situation first. Your life has to be in real danger before you shoot. It is during this period of confusion that a criminal often succeeds in taking away a victim's weapon.

We had two recent cases in San Jose where people had their guns used against them. One man and his wife were asleep when they awoke to the sound of someone trying to break into their downtown apartment. By the time the man got out of bed, found his .25-caliber automatic pistol and loaded it, it was too late. The burglar had already entered the couple's living room. When the man finally came down the stairs, the burglar overpowered him, took his gun away, shot him three times and pistol-whipped his wife.

In the other case, a woman who went home during her lunch break was shot in the chest by a burglar who had stolen her husband's gun. The intruders were neighborhood kids who were in fact looking to steal weapons.

The risk doesn't stop with your own weapon. Many gun owners get shot with another weapon. One such victim was a twenty-four-year-old San Jose man who held a party at his place for a group of friends. As the night wore on, he wanted to end the party and asked everyone to leave. When several of the partygoers refused, the host got his rifle and fired a shot in the air. He wanted to let his guests know that he meant business, and once again, he ordered them to leave. But one young man who carried a handgun pulled the weapon out and also fired one shot. This bullet, however, didn't go in the air. It killed the host.

TERRIBLE FAMILY FIGHTS

Think for a moment what might happen if, after you got into an argument with your wife, she picked up your loaded revolver. Thousands of men and women are killed or seriously injured each year in shoot-outs with their husbands, wives, boyfriends and girlfriends. I've seen so many cases where someone who has a little too much to drink blows his or her partner's head off.

You can prevent an argument from escalating into a fatal shooting by clearing your house of any weapons. A lot of people in caskets right now might not be if they had done the same thing. For example, a wealthy Texas man who bought his wife a .38-caliber gun because he wanted her to have something to protect herself with when he traveled on business. The woman defended herself just as she was taught. Unfortunately, she used the gun during a marital squabble and fired two shots that killed her husband. The couple had been married thirty-three years.

After sentencing the woman to ten years on probation, the judge in the case said: "The Mafia is not running around shooting people in the streets with handguns. It's nice people who are killing each other. You've got a handgun in the house, people get mad and say to themselves that's what it's here for—to kill somebody. You see it all the time."

In the 1950s, the members of my New York Police Academy class learned a lesson about guns that we never forgot. One of our colleagues was concerned about leaving his wife and children alone when he worked nights. He told the instructor he was going to teach her to shoot.

"For Godsakes," said the sergeant. "Never teach your wife to use a gun. Wives don't miss."

All of us in the training class laughed at that line. Everyone except the sergeant, that is. We thought he was kidding, but he was serious. He knew something we didn't—a live gun around the house is a tragedy waiting to happen. Two years later, we found out for ourselves. Another cop who was in that same training class was shot and seriously wounded by his wife, who had been suffering from severe depression.

WHAT HAPPENS WHEN YOU GET ANGRY?

I investigated many shootings in New York in which a gun, purchased for so-called protection, turned into a murder weapon. Most handgun owners don't realize that a gun can do strange things to people. Take a successful businessman who ordinarily has complete control of his emotions. If you stick a gun in his hand when he is under stress, the feeling of power can become overwhelming. This man becomes fearless. He is a different person, and his otherwise good judgment may suddenly desert him. At any moment, this killer personality can present a danger to his wife and loved ones.

I once arrested a man in New York who had blown his sister-in-law in half with a shotgun. The man was clean; he was in his mid forties, had no previous psychological problems and no criminal record. He had lost his job a month earlier, and his sister-in-law had been nagging him to find work. One day while he was cleaning his gun, a Christmas gift from a friend, the man snapped. His sister-in-law got on his case once too often and he turned the sights on her.

One reason I feel as strongly as I do about guns is that so many police officers are killed in the line of duty. A typical shooting took place in San Diego recently when two officers were fatally shot after they were called to a neighborhood disturbance. A man had complained loudly to the lady next door that a rose bush she planted was on his property. He then cursed and began hitting and kicking her. When neighbors came to assist the woman, the man ran back into his house.

Several minutes later, and without warning, the man got a semiautomatic rifle and fired 100 rounds of ammunition at police. One officer was shot through the heart. The other suffered fatal head and chest wounds. The bloody battle ended when the man walked out his front door and was killed by police bullets. All this over a rose bush. Afterward, neighbors described the man as a person who kept to himself and loved to garden. No one thought he was capable of going berserk. Nor did anyone know that he stockpiled military weapons.

YOU CAN BE ARRESTED FOR USING YOUR GUN

In California, an intruder broke into a closed business at night but ran off the premises when he was discovered by a worker. The employee charged after the burglar and shot him in the back. For this act of heroism and devotion to his employer, the man was convicted of manslaughter.

In another case, a man fell asleep shortly before a burglar broke into his home. He woke up, grabbed his gun and confronted the burglar in his house. When the burglar ran out the front door, the man shot him. He was convicted of aggravated assault.

California courts have held that deadly force may be used only when a burglary is "forcible and atrocious," one which reasonably creates a fear of death or great bodily harm. Once the suspect takes off, even with your stolen property, shooting him is against the law. In many states the use of a deadly weapon on a fleeing felon can get you thrown in jail. You can shoot only if your life or the lives of other occupants in your household are in danger.

Most burglars are unarmed, teenage kids who pose little threat. They may be little brats, but killing them carries a lot of repercussions, both legal and psychological. No matter how strongly you feel about your rights as a gun owner, you had better know the full meaning of the law.

SUPPOSING YOU DO SHOOT AND KILL SOMEONE

Many police officers suffer emotional stress and severe mental trauma after they shoot someone. In Washington state, for example, a police sergeant fell apart after he cut down a murder suspect. The cop became so paranoid that the police department declared him a danger on the streets. Even though he had no choice but to shoot, the cop could not deal with taking another life. He was forced to leave the department for more than a year.

Police shootings usually do not afford officers much time to consider alternatives. But afterward, they have all the time in the world to second-guess themselves. Many officers suffer flashbacks, nightmares and long periods of depression. Even in cases where an officer had to shoot to save his own life, he may have deep feelings of guilt. Police officers are conditioned to believe they are the good guys in society; their job is to protect human life. Yet even when the toughest-talking cop takes the life of a hardened criminal, he is likely to suffer natural feelings of remorse. The old macho illusions of the cop blowing smoke away from his gun, sticking it back in a holster and saying, "Let's go back and get a couple more," is just a myth.

All police departments reward good work. Many departments discourage shootings by rewarding officers who distinguish themselves in activities that involve risk but not the firing of a weapon—such as rescuing people from a fire, talking a gunman into releasing his hostages, or even doing volunteer work with youth groups. Good police work shouldn't focus on a cop's gun.

In San Jose, we have minimized police shootings while increasing arrests by implementing a police management system that stresses nonviolent work and downplays the heroics of shooting a felon. We have a rule that police are allowed to shoot only in defense of human life. While shooting a fleeing felon may win an officer praise in some states, it could warrant discipline in San Jose. Police officers involved in shootings in my department are rarely rewarded. Rather, they are immediately relieved of their weapons; a technical team responds to the scene and conducts a full investigation, as if the shooting were a homicide; the case is thoroughly reviewed by the internal affairs division; the officer is placed on a paid administrative leave; he has a chance to talk with a lawyer before making any statements; and he is encouraged to visit a department psychologist before coming back on duty. All of this is done for the officer's protection—it makes his transition back to the force a smooth one and eliminates any doubt in his or the public's mind that the shooting was justified.

GUNS AND ACCIDENTS

A tired cop comes home from a twelve-hour shift and joins his wife and neighbors in the backyard. He pops open a can of beer and throws some hot dogs on the barbecue grill. A few minutes later, a shot rings out from an upstairs bedroom. The cop finds his little boy slumped on the floor with a bullet through his head. His son and a neighbor's kid were playing with the cop's loaded service revolver, left in a top drawer.

Many officers have seen this tragedy unfold on a police training film. The obvious point is that no gun owner—even a police officer—can afford to get sloppy. Every cop's nightmare is to have his police revolver used to accidentally shoot someone. But as careful as we are, accidental deaths do happen.

About 2 percent of all accidental deaths in this country involve handguns, and as many as 200,000 injuries each year are caused by accidental shootings. The U.S. has paid a terrible price for its laxity in controlling these weapons. In 1979, handguns killed 58 people in Israel, 52 in Canada, 48 in Japan, 42 in West Germany, 34 in Switzerland, 21 in Sweden, 8 in Great Britain and 10,728 in the United States. Right now, a handgun death takes place in the U.S. every hour.

In Detroit, more people are killed by accidental shootings in any one year than by intruding robbers. In one year, a couple hundred children under age twelve are killed in the U.S. with handguns. Two-year-old Ricky was one of them. His father had kept a blue steel .38-caliber revolver in the top drawer of a file cabinet to protect his San Jose house from prowlers. Wearing only his diaper, Ricky sat on the family-room floor watching cartoons with his four-year-old sister and one-year-old brother.

His mother was in the kitchen sewing a shirt. His grandmother was in a bedroom asleep. His dad was at work.

Ricky crawled out of the family room, dragged a chair up to the cabinet and removed the gun from the drawer. Minutes later, the women heard the shot. They found Ricky standing rigid and bleeding from a bullet hole in the stomach. He died after three hours of surgery. The bullet had pierced Ricky's liver and passed out his back. That weekend, the family was supposed to take Ricky to Disneyland. Instead, they went to his funeral.

After the shooting, my officers found two other handguns in the file drawer—one was unregistered and the other had been reported stolen. (The boy's father had purchased the one gun without knowing it had been taken in a burglary.)

Accidents don't happen only to children. A burglary case I worked in New York showed me that adults can be just as careless. My partner knocked on the front door of an apartment. When no one answered, I climbed through the fire-escape window and searched the house. Although the burglar was gone, I noticed an elaborate pulley system attached to the window. Out of curiosity, I later asked the woman who lived there about it. Her answer ruined my day. She said her brother rigged the pulley to a double-barreled shotgun so that anyone who opened the window from the outside would get hit with a blast of pellets. Fortunately, he and his shotgun were off on a hunting trip that weekend. That was the last window I climbed through.

Owning a firearm is a major responsibility that far too many people take lightly. Frankly, having guns around the house is one of the most unpleasant aspects of my job. When I took a two-year leave of absence from the New York Police Department to attend graduate school at Harvard, I was glad to be able to raise my three young children without guns lying around.

IF YOU CHOOSE TO OWN A GUN

As much as I oppose the average person's having a gun, I recognize that some people have a legitimate need to own one. A wealthy corporate executive who fears his family might get kidnapped is one such person. A Hollywood celebrity who has to protect himself from kooks is another. If Sharon Tate had had access to a gun during the Manson killings, some innocent lives might have been saved.

However, too often too many people mistakenly think they need a gun. A merchant, for example, who makes cash deposits late at night might think his duties are good enough reason to carry a gun under his coat. What he is really asking for is a chance to exchange gunfire with a robber. Just because someone carries a lot of money doesn't mean he needs a holster. In this instance, the best protection is common sense.

First, the merchant would be wise not to go to the same bank at the same time, night after night. That way he's not a sitting duck for some robber who observes his habits.

Second, he should not get out of his car to make a deposit if he sees anyone who looks suspicious. The deposit can wait a while.

Third, he shouldn't carry the money in a paper sack. Use a bag that has a lock. And the merchant shouldn't let others know that he deposits large amounts of cash at night.

For homeowners, I recommend they invest the price of a handgun toward the cost of installing a burglar alarm or buying a watchdog. These measures will make your resistance much safer than having a handgun lying around.

If despite my best advice you still want to own a gun, you need to know how to properly store one. Remember that a gun, like a burglar alarm, is not a substitute for taking basic security precautions such as installing dead-bolt locks and peepholes.

If you must own a gun, follow these rules:

1. Know the laws in your state concerning when you can use a gun.
2. Take professional lessons on how to shoot a gun.
3. Plan in advance how you will get to your gun and use it in case of emergency.

4. If you have children, or a spouse who does not know how to handle a gun, you must safeguard it. I suggest you keep all weapons unloaded, with the ammunition in a separate location. In the case of a revolver, place a lock through the open cylinder. On an automatic, a guard should be used to prevent the trigger from being pulled. A rifle and shotgun are best stored if the safety bar is put through the trigger mechanism.

What good is a weapon if it is locked and unloaded? Not much. Only you can decide how readily available you want to make your weapon to yourself, your children and burglars. If you fear night intruders, for example, you might want to be like Nancy Reagan and keep your weapon under your pillow or mattress. In fact, under your bed is not such a bad location in the day, either, provided you don't have curious little kids running around your house. Another excellent hiding place for a handgun is in a wall receptacle or inside the base of a large lamp.

Because of the nature of my job and some threats I have received, I keep a loaded weapon close to me at night. But I never have a gun in the house when I'm not there. I am very careful because I know how I'd feel if my weapon were stolen and used to kill an innocent person. You too should consider this when deciding how to store your gun.

If you have a sophisticated burglar alarm system or an alert watchdog you may not need to unload your gun and put a safety lock on it. If, however, you don't have any means of warning should an intruder approach your house, you need to be more concerned about someone easily finding a loaded weapon and using it against you.

If you want a handgun, you have the legal right in most states to purchase one. Normally, you must fill out an application for a permit at your police department. A license is not required to keep a gun in your home or business. In most states, a license is not required to carry a rifle or shotgun. The only restriction is that you may not carry these weapons loaded in certain places.

In many cities, you must demonstrate a need to carry a handgun. A few cities—the number is growing—have passed legislation prohibiting residents from legally owning handguns. Your ability to obtain a gun permit varies depending on where you live. In San Jose, I have made it considerably tougher for residents to get handgun permits. In the past, a citizen who had no criminal background or record of psychological problems stood a good chance of getting a permit. Now, my department requires proof that there is a need; proof that the person knows the law; and proof that he knows how to fire a weapon. He also must submit to an extensive background investigation.

When it comes to choosing a weapon, you have three basic options: a handgun, rifle or shotgun. You should discuss these choices with a reputable gun dealer or your local police department. A handgun is the most convenient of the three. It is so small it can fit into a coat pocket, a purse or a bedroom drawer. While a handgun does not have the power of a rifle, it is deadly accurate at short range. To fire a rifle you need to be physically strong. Unlike a handgun, a rifle is fired from the shoulder. Like a handgun, it requires some training and expertise to operate. I advise against using rifles for protection, unless you live somewhere in the Rocky Mountains, in which case you already know more about rifles than I do. A shotgun is the most deadly and accurate weapon available. You simply can't miss at close range. The sight of the weapon alone can be an awesome deterrent. Police officers have found that the jacking of a shell into the chamber of a shotgun is usually enough in itself to frighten some people into surrendering.

If you are ever forced to fire a weapon, always aim for the midsection, or trunk area. Forget about that TV stuff of clipping someone in the arm or leg. If you feel justified in causing only a flesh wound, you've got no business pulling the trigger. Police are trained to aim for the trunk because it provides the largest target and the chance of missing is less. I do not intend to give shooting lessons here. If you are serious about owning a gun, see a professional instructor. Shooting is not something you learn overnight by reading a few pages in a book. It requires lessons and plenty of target practice.

As far as handguns are concerned, I'm convinced that I wouldn't be alive today if New York's strong gun laws hadn't discouraged people from carrying handguns while I worked the streets.

There is no evidence that owning a handgun is a deterrent to crime, and I think the opposite is true. Roughly 90 percent of crimes involving guns are committed with handguns. If anything, a handgun in the home creates an incentive for someone to steal it. By banning handguns, we could significantly decrease the criminal's ability to get a weapon. The question boils down to how real is the need of the law-abiding citizen to have a handgun versus the risk of having it fall into the hands of criminals.

Even if we were to pass a moratorium tomorrow on all newly manufactured handguns, it would take many years before all guns were taken away from criminals. But if we don't stop, estimates are that we will have 90 million guns by the year 2000—nearly twice as many as are already in circulation.

Sooner or later we're going to have to come to grips with the problem. For now, I just can't believe that so many people feel they have to become gunslingers to feel safe in our society.

4

SELF-DEFENSE . . .
FANTASY AND REALITY

A New York police officer used to walk around the station swiping his arms at imaginary opponents and kicking his legs in midair. Whenever anyone asked the officer what on earth he was doing, he boasted about his years of martial-arts training: "God help the poor SOB who has to face one of my lethal karate blows."

Half of the officers on the force were convinced that this guy's karate kick was deadly. The others thought he was a big phony.

One day, the officer finally got a chance to test his flaunted skills. A dispatcher sent him to midtown Manhattan to check a report of a psycho creating a public disturbance. A man about 5 feet 5 inches tall and 150 pounds was jumping up and down, screaming and carrying on in the street as if it were New Year's Eve in Times Square. Actually, it was June and the deranged man was holding up traffic.

The officer made several attempts to subdue him before exerting some physical force. Then came the feared karate blow to the neck. A pair of backup units arrived in the nick of time to see the little man get to his feet and punch the cop's lights out. The psycho then fought off five uniformed officers before he was handcuffed and taken into custody.

From that day on, we never heard another peep out of the police department's embarrassed martial-arts master.

A similar case in San Jose involved a powerful young officer who kept himself in top physical shape by lifting weights five times a week. The cop tried to restrain a skinny teenager who was flipping out on the drug PCP. During the struggle, the doped-up kid took away the officer's baton and nearly beat him to death. As the patrolman drifted into unconsciousness, he reached for his gun and shot the youth. Had he not pulled the trigger when he did, the cop would have bled to death.

No matter how much you train in self-defense, you cannot expect to control every individual who crosses your path. Sometimes years of martial-arts training, six months of study in a police academy, and weight lifting are not enough to restrain a psycho whose adrenaline is flowing sky-high, or a youth tripping out on mind-altering drugs. Neither, I discovered, did the various police holds I learned in the academy always work on suspects, who weren't nearly as cooperative as my training partner. Like many officers, I discovered the hard way that self-defense techniques are sometimes useless. These holds depend on inflicting pain to subdue an opponent. Unfortunately, some people who abuse drugs feel no pain. Then what?

If you have graduated from a rigorous physical-training program, don't be misled into thinking you are indestructible. I don't want to discourage you from enrolling in self-defense or karate classes, because they can be extremely helpful in building confidence and teaching you effective self-defense. However, many of these programs are billed as the next best thing to carrying a gun. You should know that no weapons training or self-defense course can turn you into an Incredible Hulk.

I have seen a number of instructional manuals that purport to teach readers how to physically overcome a criminal. These are guides printed by organizations ranging from the federal government to fly-by-night firms that are out to make a quick buck. There are those that come complete with pictures of an Angie Dickinson look-alike wearing a dress and high heels. Some show a woman thrusting an umbrella in front of herself like a bayonet, using keys to thwart off an attacker and squeezing a container of lemon juice in an assailant's face. They also recommend the following tips for women to use against attackers:

Carry everyday items to use as weapons: a pen or pencil, red pepper, lemon juice, a key ring or an umbrella.

Attack an assailant at his throat, stomach, temples, eyes or kneecaps.

Use a knee to the groin if an assailant makes an attack from the front.

Use an elbow to give an assailant a sharp blow to the stomach if attacked from the rear.

Stomp on the other person's foot at the instep as a defensive measure.

Women who read this kind of garbage and think they can safely defend themselves are really being taken for a ride. Frankly, anyone who follows this junk could end up getting themselves killed. If you're the type of person who has little confidence in your ability to fight back, then by all means you should enroll in a self-defense course. But don't rely on a manual or magazine article to tell you how it is done.

THE IDEA IS TO ESCAPE

The most important piece of advice when defending yourself is to remember what I've been saying throughout this book: Your goal is to *escape*. No more. You do not want to even think about inflicting pain on your attacker until you've exhausted all efforts to flee. So many self-defense manuals tell people how to fight back without ever mentioning that violence often is not necessary to get away.

Escaping is where the citizen has a major advantage over a police officer. The cop on the street has to take people into custody, even if they put up a fight. You, on the other hand, don't have to stick around and conquer. Your only concern is breaking free. You should only use physical force as a last resort, and if you do, go for broke. Don't play around with pouring red pepper in someone's eyes or squeezing lemon juice in his face. You want to disable an attacker long enough so you can get away.

As much as I'm against giving advice on how to physically defend yourself in a book, there are a couple of maneuvers I learned in police training that I have found to be invaluable.

BALANCE AND QUICKNESS

Whenever a police officer frisks and handcuffs a suspect, he is trained to order the suspect to stand on his toes and lean against a wall or the side of a squad car, supporting himself on his fingertips. Do you know why? So that in case the suspect suddenly turns around, the officer can knock him off his feet with a swift forearm or leg kick. The same technique can be applied to defending yourself against an attacker. The trick is for you to maintain good balance while keeping your opponent off balance. To do this, lean slightly forward on the balls of your feet with your arms raised. You don't want to get caught flat-footed, standing up straight or with your hands behind your back. Once you have mastered the ready position, don't attempt to match your strength and power straight up against an assailant's. Instead, use your balance and leverage to surprise him. Provided your attacker is not armed, you can get the upper hand by using your personal weapons on his vulnerable areas. By personal weapons, I mean the front and back part of your head (for butting); your fingers, flexed slightly and held rigid (for a painful jab); a stiff elbow thrown at shoulder height; a short, snappy kick to a shin, knee or groin.

The human body has a number of spots that are particularly vulnerable to swift blows. The most vulnerable parts, such as the liver, stomach, ribs or groin, are located on or near the midline. Knowing where to strike someone and apply pain is just as important as knowing how to overtake them. Many people instinctively go for the face, even though that is where most of us expect to get hit first. Instead, go after large, unprotected areas such as the stomach, groin or thighs.

STAY COOL, BE CLEVER

If an assailant is armed, you need to keep your cool and think your options through. Try to talk him out of using a gun by telling him it isn't really necessary. Then grab the first opportunity to run away. But remember that you can't outrun a bullet. If an attacker has a knife, don't even think of trying a TV stunt such as knocking the weapon away with a spectacular karate kick. Again, my advice is to buy time using subterfuge until you see a chance to break away. Obviously, if you can locate a hammer, a lead pipe or any other similar hard object, you're better off than if you must rely on your personal weapons alone. In that case, one of the most effective blows is to smash an object against the inside of your assailant's shins. That should give you time to escape.

So, if you should ever face potential physical danger, try the following: assess the situation (can you run away, scream for help, etc.); size up the assailant (is he 6'2", 245 pounds or 5'2", 110 pounds); and determine your own ability to function in an emergency (are you capable of using a particular move without hesitating).

A DIFFERENT KIND OF ATTACKER

Less serious but sometimes equally frightening crimes are obscene and threatening phone calls. Many people, especially women, feel defenseless when they are subjected to repeated crank calls.

I do not know of a single obscene caller who actually carried through his threats. For these people, the act of making the calls is usually enough to satisfy their sick minds. Fortunately, obscene phone calls are relatively easy to trace. Working with the phone company, the police frequently pick up obscene callers at their addresses minutes after they have completed a call.

Still, obscene phone calls can be just as scary as a physical threat. The police view these callers as potentially dangerous because many of them are sex offenders. Most of the time, though, the caller is known to the victim. It could be an angry spouse, a jilted boyfriend, a former business partner, etc. The caller can be a respected member of the community. Recently in suburban San Jose, a school administrator was convicted of threatening a twelve-year-old girl over the phone. The administrator told the girl she was going to die after she had tried to halt his romantic advances toward her mother. The mother and daughter, who suffers from cancer, filed a $3 million civil lawsuit against the man for intentional infliction of emotional distress.

Here are seven steps you can take to thwart obscene telephone callers:

1. Hang up immediately and call police. Don't panic or lose control of your senses. Obscene phone calls are not uncommon.

2. If the calls continue over a long period of time, change your telephone number.

3. If a caller asks what number he dialed, don't tell him. Ask him what number he is calling. Whatever you do, don't give your phone number to a stranger. Many obscene callers pick up the phone and dial seven random digits. So don't give him a chance to look up your address by giving him your phone number.

4. Do not tell the caller where you live. By doing so, you only encourage him to carry out his threats.

5. Immediately hand the phone to your husband or another man in the house. Most, if not all, obscene callers are male and do not get the same thrill out of intimidating men.

6. If you're a woman living by yourself or with a female roommate, have a male friend tape a recorded message on an answering machine.

7. If calls are repeated, keep a whistle by the phone. When the freak calls, blow the whistle into the phone as loud as you can. Primitive as it sounds, you'll batter his eardrum, and shatter his disturbed fantasy. This is an effective way of discouraging another call.

5

RANDOM VIOLENCE . . .
TERRIBLE BUT NOT ALWAYS SO RANDOM

Joe Jackson sat down with his family to enjoy a Thanksgiving Day turkey. Then he heard a knock at the front door. As he got up from the table, Jackson had no idea who was waiting on his porch. He certainly did not expect a teenager carrying a pistol. Poor Jackson never had a chance. He opened the door, saw that the youth was armed and tried to flick the ashes from his cigarette in the kid's face. The attempt was futile. The young robber pulled the trigger and killed Jackson instantly.

Joe Jackson was the first murder victim during my police administration in Kansas City. He had survived three decades as an ambulance driver, a dangerous job that required him to respond to bloody murders and freeway accidents and make countless high-speed trips to the hospital. At age fifty-nine, he looked forward to retirement and a peaceful life with his wife and kids. Two weeks after he left his job he was gunned down in his own house by a teenaged killer.

Rick Patterson was hitchhiking to his suburban Los Angeles home to help his sister prepare for her upcoming wedding. After only a few minutes of waving his thumb at oncoming traffic, the pleasant-looking eighteen-year-old was picked up by two men in a green Ford van. The three exchanged greetings and the conversation quickly turned to sex. The driver asked Patterson if he liked gays. Patterson said he was bisexual and agreed to ride to the driver's house, where the three would go to bed together.

In the course of sex, Patterson was tied up and strangled with his own T-shirt. His nude corpse was later found ditched behind a gas station. Patterson was one of a reported sixteen victims of William Bonin, better known as the ritualistic "Freeway Killer." (Much of the information on Patterson came from Bonin's partner, who pleaded guilty to a lesser charge and received a lighter sentence in exchange for cooperating with authorities.)

Every day, Robert Townes walked from his Columbia University office at 116th Street to the train station at 125th Street in New York, despite warnings from students and colleagues. They knew Harlem was not a safe area, so they cautioned him not to walk through the neighborhood alone. But Townes, a highly respected professor at Columbia, had walked that same route for dozens of years. He was not about to allow the fears of his friends to alter his routine. One day, Townes was held up and stabbed to death.

Frank Garcia was leaving a San Jose shopping center with his two-year-old son, Frank III, when they were approached by a thirty-four-year-old man posing as a female police officer. The phony cop wore a blond wig, maroon stretch slacks and a blouse with two bunched-up pieces of cloth taped to his chest. Four hours later, worried relatives found Garcia and his son inside their blue van. Garcia was dead of ten stab wounds and his little boy had a slit neck and was gasping for air. Also inside was the transvestite, who had been shot to death.

My detectives believed the bloodbath happened this way: the transvestite forced Garcia and his son into the van at gunpoint. Once inside, he snapped handcuffs on the father's wrists, then put his pistol down in the van to get undressed. At that point, the father grabbed the gun and squeezed off four shots. As the transvestite struggled to stay alive, he repeatedly plunged a Buck knife into Garcia's neck, face and chest. In a final act of rage, he drew the knife across the young boy's neck.

Pete Little was an extremely popular landlord. He took care of his tenants as if they were his family. On the first of every month he personally went door to door to collect the rent and pass out candy to the children. Little's friends warned him that he was offering himself as a sitting duck. Everyone in the building knew he came around at the same time every month. They also knew he collected lots of cash. But Little dismissed the potential danger. He wanted to serve his tenants and keep his property in good shape. To him, the best way to do this was to collect the rent and inspect the property himself. A robber shot Little to death one day as he made his monthly rounds.

A surprise attack by a total stranger is perhaps the most frightening crime of all. It's called random violence. That's exactly what killed the retired ambulance driver, the hitchhiker, the Columbia professor, the man with his little boy and the landlord. In each case, the victim lost his life because he was in the wrong spot at the wrong time. Call it fate, rotten luck, whatever. It could just as easily have been your life or mine.

CUTTING YOUR RISKS

None of the five deaths, however, was truly random: All five victims could have avoided a confrontation with their killers. I'm not saying the victims deserved to die or that they were to blame for their deaths. Far from it. Each of the five murders was a gruesome act by a killer or killers who ought to be hanged. But in each case the victim could have sidestepped his own death trap.

Take the retired ambulance driver. Had he installed an inexpensive peephole in his apartment door, he would have seen a young stranger armed with a gun. He would never have opened that door. But he didn't have the peephole, and since it was Thanksgiving Day, the ambulance driver obviously felt he had no reason to fear danger.

When someone knocks on your door, regardless of where you live, don't open it without first seeing who's there. If you rent an apartment or house, you can force your landlord to install security devices such as peepholes and dead-bolt locks. If you own your home, spend a couple of bucks this weekend to put in a peephole.

Take the high school student. His life was snuffed out by sadistic killers who enjoyed strangling young boys. Do you think the gay youth would have been killed if he hadn't been hitch-hiking on that balmy June day? Of course not. If the young man had taken a bus to his sister's place instead of hitchhiking, he would be alive today. It's a risky business when you thumb a ride or pick up a hitchhiker. You assume the other person is someone you can trust.

Take the Columbia University professor. He may have been a scholar, but he didn't use everyday common sense. He felt his friends and colleagues who warned him not to walk through Harlem had become victims of hysteria. "I've been walking these streets for years, and nothing's ever happened to me yet," he told them. Well, times had changed and so had those streets. If you learn that a neighborhood is unsafe, stay away.

Take the San Jose father and his little boy. The transvestite was a low-life criminal who had been arrested in four states for armed robbery, forgery, theft and drug dealing. What he did to that little boy and his father is beyond comprehension. Just as sad is the fact that the father was unable to avoid the transvestite in the grocery-store parking lot. Earlier that same day at a nearby shopping center, the transvestite approached an elderly couple in the same manner. The minute they saw the transvestite walking toward them, the couple suspected something wasn't right. The old woman scared him off by blowing a whistle. Unfortunately, the father did not sense that same danger until it was too late. If he had, he and his boy might have escaped also.

Take the Harlem landlord. He really should have known better. I could understand his motives, if he had been collecting rent from farmers in Topeka. But here he was in the middle of the city's highest crime area taking cash from residents at the same time on the same day every month. He was setting himself up. His friends and relatives worried about him, but they couldn't alter his actions. "You don't understand," he told them. "These people can be trusted. They are my tenants."

So, again, although these five murders were random, each of them could have been avoided. Follow the advice in this chapter and you will all but eliminate the chances of meeting a similar fate.

RISK AND YOUR LIFESTYLE

A recent FBI study found that each of us has a 1-in-157 chance of becoming a murder victim. According to the Justice Department, more than half of all violent crimes are committed by strangers. Those two figures are enough to scare anyone. But when you break both numbers down, truly random violence just isn't that widespread.

The 1-in-157 ratio includes victims who are part of youth gangs who roam ghetto streets, criminals who regularly deal in prostitution and drugs, and gun owners who have a history of alcohol abuse or severe mental problems. It also includes promiscuous gays and straights, hitchhikers, liquor-store clerks and bartenders. All of these people are more likely to become victims of violent crime than those of us who stay away from risky occupations and neighborhoods.

Thus, the chances of becoming a victim of random violence vary according to your lifestyle. A recent *People* magazine story, for example, reported the number of handgun deaths in the United States during a twenty-four-hour period. The story said that forty-two people were murdered and twenty-eight committed suicide. Twenty-seven handgun deaths involved quarrels of some kind, four were part of robbery attempts and two resulted from drug deals that went awry. Causes of the nine other deaths were unknown. That means, of the forty-two deaths, none was truly random. If you do not serve drinks in a bar, abuse alcohol, hitchhike or push drugs, your chances of facing a violent criminal are slim. But the chances are not zero, regardless of your lifestyle.

When I worked as a street cop in New York, two teams of officers were gunned down on patrol. The first pair was shot in the back while walking near a housing project at the site of the Polo Grounds, once the baseball home of the New York Giants. A year later, a second team of officers was murdered on routine patrol in lower Manhattan. Even though these four police officers were armed and dressed in uniform, they didn't have a chance. They were simply the victims of random attacks in broad daylight. There was nothing they could do.

The same set of circumstances took the life of a San Jose man recently as he ate lunch with his wife at a Big Boy's restaurant. Seated in a car parked across the street was a man who fired a single shot at the diner. The bullet hit the victim, a fifty-four-year-old father of two, in the chest and killed him. He did not know his killer, who was a thirty-seven-year-old air force veteran and former mental patient. After his arrest, the suspect told a court psychiatrist that he shot and killed the man because he was following the instructions of a voice on the car radio. "I was cued on the radio," he said. "The announcer kept making hints. This and that." On the day of the murder, the killer recalled, he pulled up to a stoplight in front of the restaurant when a voice on the car radio said, "That's him in the white shirt." So he grabbed his hunting rifle, slipped a shell into the chamber and zeroed in on the man's chest. One shot was all it took.

We can all be thankful that these cases are extremely rare. Unless you adopt the lifestyle of a monk, you can't protect yourself against someone as crazy as that air force veteran. But I don't want to scare you into thinking these kinds of random attacks occur all the time. Lord knows the media does enough of that already. When people learn the details of a sensational murder from the newspapers or television, they often get anxious about the safety of their neighborhood, especially if the crime occurred nearby.

What these people don't realize is that the media leave out important details of many crimes because they don't know them. A classic example is a brutal murder several years ago that terrified an entire New York community. The nude body of a popular, middle-aged deacon who served a Catholic parish was found bound and gagged in his own apartment. The man had been tortured to death. The next day, a monsignor publicly denounced the violence and demanded that the police do something immediately. As expected, Mayor John Lindsay responded by putting tremendous pressure on the police to catch the killer.

The shouts of outrage by the monsignor and the mayor attracted wide media coverage. Within twenty-four hours police discovered the deacon led a secret life that no one knew of. He was a promiscuous homosexual who frequently picked up young boys and brought them back to his apartment. On this occasion, he brought someone home who was more interested in violence than sex.

When the monsignor learned of this, he stopped making inflammatory remarks about the police department. His comments that people were no longer safe in their houses also came to a halt. To spare the victim, his family and the monsignor any embarrassment, the details of the deacon's lifestyle were not exposed in the media. What New Yorkers thought was a random mutilation case that could happen to anyone, actually was something very different.

Police frequently learn during the course of an investigation that a victim was a dope dealer, a prostitute, a pimp or a member of organized crime. But unless the police chief is running for mayor, we don't routinely hold press conferences to announce the sordid details. We don't want to attract a potential libel suit, nor do we want to hamper an investigation by upsetting the victim's family or friends. When police do release details in murder cases, they are accused of being lacking in sympathy for the victim's family. The police have to be sensitive to critics who claim that we don't work as hard on cases involving so-called second-class citizens: prostitutes, pimps, etc. After all, a questionable lifestyle does not justify murder.

So the next time you read about a particularly vicious crime, don't be misled. Remember that if the victim went from bar to bar trying to score with a prostitute before he was killed, you probably won't read about it in your local newspaper.

USE COMMON SENSE

Rash or stubborn behavior puts many people in danger. They are not necessarily to blame for getting hurt, but their actions are partly responsible for their troubles.

You do not, for example, want to be a Three-Martini Hero, like the two men I mentioned earlier who were robbed one night after leaving a fashionable restaurant with their wives. Believing themselves to be real-life superheroes, thanks to their alcoholic courage, they chased the armed youths. The robbers turned around and shot both men, badly wounding one and crippling the other.

Here's a less extreme approach to that kind of situation, not as heroic perhaps, but saner. A few years ago, my cousin, his wife, my wife and I were walking to a San Francisco restaurant when two thugs tried to snatch a handbag from my cousin's wife. Neither robber appeared to be armed, so my cousin and I chased them down a narrow street. We trapped one of them on the second floor of a dark parking structure. I was off duty, out of my jurisdiction, without my gun and did not know for certain whether the robber was carrying a weapon. Since I was unwilling to risk my life over an attempted larceny, I decided to retreat and rejoin the two women.

My advice is not to chase after anyone unless you are confident you can physically overtake them. As a veteran policeman, I pursued these kids instinctively. Had I caught up with them in the street, I would have relied on my professional experience to overcome them. But when I lost sight of them, I was satisfied to notify police. In short, I was more concerned about my safety than making a minor arrest. The Three-Martini Heroes, on the other hand, were determined to catch the youths even though they knew at least one of them was armed.

BE A COWARD—DON'T STRIKE BACK

Random violence often occurs when two strangers become involved in an altercation. Whether it's an argument over who gets to use a barroom pool table or who is entitled to a parking place, most fights start because one party is not mature enough to back off.

Our nation's highways are one of the most common sites of

violence today. The following scenario is so familiar: one driver cuts off another; the two exchange heated words; someone pulls out a gun.

My advice is to act like a coward and go home. If something happens that you feel strongly about, call the police. But don't be a child. Don't yell at people, give them the finger or honk your horn. Just shrug and be on your way, and enjoy the feeling of superiority, that you are above such adolescent foolishness.

STAY OUT OF DANGER ZONES

Some years ago a private transit company that conducted bus tours of New York City warned visitors to stay away from Harlem. The mayor of New York at the time, John Lindsay, chastised the touring company for making such offhanded and degrading remarks about certain sections of the city.

I didn't agree with the mayor then, and I still don't. Just about every large city in the United States has a high-crime area. And although advising tourists to stay away from these areas may have political and racial overtones, it can prevent serious injury and property losses.

Whenever you visit another city, find out what sections of town are considered unsafe and those that aren't. Tourists who naively wander into high-crime areas and get robbed are victims not so much of random violence as of their own carelessness.

Many people resist moving out of high-crime areas because they refuse to be run out of town by hoodlums. For years my cousin and his wife lived in a beautiful, low-rent Manhattan apartment house. They loved the location because it was close to all the restaurants, stores and theaters in Manhattan. Because of this, they refused to heed my advice to move out. I patrolled that area as a street cop, and I knew it was one of the most dangerous in New York. Even though they had alarms, locks and a dog, their apartment was burglarized several times.

They persisted in their stubbornness for a number of years. One day I was surprised to learn they had finally decided to move. They said the final straw came when a burglar murdered the couple who lived one floor beneath them. My cousin, who is a criminologist, was one of the last persons in the neighborhood to move out. Since nothing worse than burglary ever happened to him, he also was among the luckiest.

6

PASTIMES, PLEASURES AND DANGERS

Throughout this book I have stressed the importance of installing dead-bolt locks on your doors, jogging in safe areas and during daylight hours, and avoiding rowdy bars. These precautions won't mean a thing, however, if you engage in risky pastimes and pleasures. Many crime victims learn, after it is too late, that by altering their lifestyles they could have avoided contact with vicious criminals. Until now, you probably thought it was harmless for someone to spend a Friday night with a prostitute or at a local gambling parlor. But, in fact, such activities can be extremely dangerous.

GAMBLING

High-stakes betting can be found in most U.S. cities. Often the game is among friends who meet every weekend; maybe it's an organized operation run at a local pool hall. Most players in organized gambling games do not realize they put themselves in considerable danger every time they sit at a table. They know that gambling is illegal and they risk losing a considerable chunk of money. What they don't realize is that gambling houses are a haven for armed robbers. Where else does so much cash change hands out of sight of police? Also, by participating in an illegal activity, gamblers remove themselves from the protection of the law.

To protect their clients, many gambling establishments do not permit strangers inside. The Wah Mee Club in Seattle's

Chinatown took such precautions. To enter the parlor, members had to ring a buzzer and go through three sets of heavy locked doors equipped with peepholes. The locks automatically engaged and opened from the inside, where an attendant seated in a cage was always on duty. Unfortunately, the strong security measures didn't stop three young Oriental men one night from committing the worst mass killing in Seattle history.

Two of the men pulled handguns on fourteen people socializing around gaming tables, where as much as $10,000 was known to change hands in an hour. As one man bound ten of the victims—most were restaurant owners and employees—another emptied their pockets, scattered their personal belongings across the room and took their cash. Then, the two gunmen shot all fourteen people, most of them in the head. The one survivor crawled into a back alley and tipped police to the slayings inside. There was so much blood and gore inside the club that police officers said they were in danger of slipping on the floor, a grisly experience I've known once or twice in my career.

After hearing accounts of such gruesome slayings, many people think of the poor, helpless victims inside that club. But had the victims not occupied the gambling joint to begin with, they would not have been killed. High-stakes gambling parlors are not safe entertainment spots.

PROSTITUTION

Paul Kennedy was returning home one day when he decided to pull off the freeway and drive downtown. He circled the area of Fifth and Reed Streets several times for a quick peek at the big-busted ladies in gym shorts and high-heeled shoes. The neighborhood is a well-known haven for prostitutes in San Jose.

Paul didn't plan on picking anyone up. His wife was expecting him soon, and besides, he was short on cash. But when two women approached his car, Paul let them in and drove for several blocks to a secluded parking lot where he had sex with one of the women in the backseat. The other sat in front puffing on a cigarette. Paul apparently didn't keep a close eye on the second woman, because the next day he noticed that $3,000 worth of jewelry was missing from underneath the front seat of the car. Since prostitutes don't give receipts, Paul had no way of knowing who ripped him off. He was hesitant to report the theft to police because he, too, had engaged in an illegal act. But he was so angry that he had been taken by the prostitutes, he reported the crime anyway.

So many people think they protect their valuables by hiding them under a car seat. That's ridiculous. Paul thought his property was safe because the sex act took place in his car. Obviously, he didn't have his eyes on the jewelry. We never discovered why Paul decided to take on two prostitutes. Perhaps he wanted to soothe his ego a bit. Whatever the reason, he wasn't aware that prostitutes commonly work in pairs—one diverts the victim's attention, while the other takes his valuables.

A prostitute's partner isn't always another woman. Recently, a twenty-four-year-old San Jose man met a young woman in a West Side bar. After buying her a few drinks, he talked her into letting him take her home. The man thought his charm and wit had impressed the young woman so much that she was willing to have sex with him. Of course, he didn't know that she was a prostitute and had planned the encounter from the time he first walked into the bar. Nor did he imagine how she worked her trade. When they got to her place, the couple had another drink and sex before the man left, shortly after midnight. The woman never spoke of money. The next day the man was startled and a bit embarrassed to find that his car had been broken into and $500 was missing. By the time he reported the crime to police, he still hadn't realized that he was set up by a clever man-and-woman team. It turned out that the prostitute and her partner had quite a business going. She took her men home and picked their pockets, while he collected valuables from their vehicles. They only selected customers who drove fancy cars or flashed large wads of cash.

More often, though, prostitutes work together in simpler scams. And they go after anyone who has something worth stealing. Phillip Burns, thirty-seven, was drinking a beer one weekday afternoon in an empty downtown San Jose tavern when two rather attractive young women approached him. Phil had been confined to a wheelchair since he was stricken with polio as a youth, and it did not occur to him at first that the two girls were professional prostitutes. Nor did it really matter. When one of the women negotiated a price for sex, he gladly accepted. The two ladies got into his specially equipped van and drove to an apartment-complex parking lot, where their services were rendered.

Phil later told police that he paid $30 for oral sex. Prostitutes often demand payment in advance so their customers will be hesitant to tell police they knowingly engaged in illegal sex acts. But Phil came to police after he discovered that $140 in cash was missing from his trousers' pocket. With Phil's help, both women were arrested on the streets.

This is just another example of what happens when you put yourself in the company of criminals. Yes, believe it or not, prostitutes are definitely criminals, though you'd never know it by the way the media and entertainment business portray these "ladies" as glamorous personalities. Prostitutes are often presented on the silver screen as sincere, hardworking women with hearts of gold. To the police officer who encounters them day in and day out, the practice of glorifying and romanticizing prostitution as an all-American sport is a farce. He knows that most hookers are vicious, violent criminals. All that interests them are a potential customer and his money.

Don't ever let anyone sucker you into believing that if more states legalized prostitution, the number of rapes would be cut in half. The only ones who would benefit are the hookers themselves and their pimps. Prostitutes are involved in illegal activities that go far beyond unlawful sex. Some have serious narcotics habits and steal to pay for their fix. They are pressured by their pimps to score, which doesn't mean just landing a customer; it also entails stealing to get more than the fee. Don't be so naive as to think the lucrative part of being a hooker is raking in fifty bucks for a quick pop. The real money is in taking their customers for everything they can.

Besides protecting your livelihood and your pocketbook, there are some other more practical reasons why people should steer clear of prostitutes. Many, of course, carry infectious diseases that can cause serious health problems. In addition, many cities that are plagued with prostitution problems use decoy officers of both sexes to lure prostitutes and their customers, better known in the trade as "johns." I have seen the careers of too many clergymen, corporate presidents, school administrators, newspaper editors, judges and a host of other respected individuals destroyed after they were arrested for "negotiating" with a female officer. Such an arrest, of course, also causes tremendous embarrassment to family members. The Oakland city council recently began reading the names of individuals arrested for soliciting prostitutes at its meetings. Also, you should know that many judges are giving automatic jail sentences to prostitutes and their customers. In San Jose, johns face a two-day jail sentence for the first offense.

With the risk of injury, theft, disease, unwanted publicity and a jail term, you had better think twice about buying sex.

BARS

In the rape chapter, I warned women to be careful about going home with strange men. I said they shouldn't feel they have to stay out of bars completely as long as they were careful. The same goes for men. I'm not campaigning to put taverns out of business, but you should know that bars are not as safe as the neighborhood grocery store. They remain open late at night, have large amounts of cash on hand and are dark inside, all attractive elements to the armed robber.

A look at three barroom robbers, who were finally caught by my department, shows what dangerous hangouts taverns can be. The men, two of whom were brothers from southern California, were arrested for committing a string of barroom holdups in several western states. Before they were caught in San Jose, the brothers had been released early from five-year-to-life sentences in state prison for a 1975 conviction on robbery and assault to commit murder charges.

They were captured in San Jose after a hostage incident. One night around ten, the three men walked into a bar wearing masks and carrying guns. They forced the patrons to lie on the floor and took their wallets, purses and jewelry. One of the men fired two shots from a handgun, striking a customer in the thigh. By the time the trio was ready to leave, my officers had surrounded the bar. For the next five hours, police negotiated with the men until they tried to escape by mingling with released hostages.

After we booked the three men into county jail, we discovered that they had also shot and nearly murdered a San Jose police officer, in connection with yet another earlier tavern robbery—obviously their specialty.

You should be aware of the dangers that can surface in a bar. Carefully select the taverns you frequent. By the nature of their location and their clientele, certain bars are more likely to attract undesirables than others. You can, for instance, predict trouble in a joint that erupts in barroom brawls every Saturday night.

GAY LIFESTYLE

Numerous police reports have shown that promiscuous homosexuals are among the most common targets of vicious beatings in this country. It's unclear whether this relates only to the gay population or if it applies equally to promiscuous straights. One thing is for sure: for decades certain groups and individuals have considered it perfectly legitimate to prey on homosexuals. Many major cities have "rat packs" that roam parks and other places where homosexuals congregate for the sole purpose of pummeling gays. Some of these youth gangs have even murdered.

I remember the time three male joggers were found clubbed to death in a New York City park. At first, police couldn't figure out why they were killed. Robbery was not the motive because the men carried no credit cards or cash. Their backgrounds were clean and they worked in perfectly legitimate jobs. For a while, we thought that perhaps these poor guys just happened to meet some sick punks who beat them to death for no apparent reason. But that happens so infrequently that no one connected with the case believed it. Finally, further investigation uncovered the facts—the three men were gays who were stopped by a gang of youths carrying baseball bats. Details of the killings were never made clear, but it seems the victims did nothing to provoke the attack other than run through a section of the park where homosexuals were known to congregate. These kinds of assaults are by no means strange occurrences in major cities with large gay populations, such as New York or San Francisco.

Today gays find that they are a special target much as blacks were for many years in the deep South. One way gays can protect themselves is not to socialize with total strangers who may turn out to be violent criminals in disguise. Like Jack the Ripper, who preyed on prostitutes, there have been a number of killers who have sought out and tortured promiscuous gays. The reasons vary—some killers have latent or actual homosexual tendencies that they are unable to cope with. Others are psychologically disturbed. Whatever the reason, gays need to be aware that such dangerous people exist and that a promiscuous lifestyle increases the chance of attack. Remember the New York deacon in the chapter on random violence who was found dead in his apartment after he brought home a sex partner, or the many victims of the Freeway Killer in Los Angeles. These are just two of many instances where gays paid dearly for their promiscuity.

Another practice among gays that sometimes leads to violence is engaging in sadism and masochism, better known as S&M. Last year, Californians were startled by a San Francisco newspaper story which reported that the county coroner had disclosed that 10 percent of the city's homicides were the result of S&M sex acts. The newspaper further reported that the coroner was starting a unique crime-prevention effort by conducting classes on safe S&M techniques. The coroner has since denied parts of the report and filed a lawsuit against the newspaper, charging that the story destroyed his career. Whatever the precise figures, it is quite obvious that any sex act that involves the use of violent force or the binding of one partner makes serious injury or death a real possibility. The fact that some people routinely engage in S&M for sexual pleasure occasionally shows up on police homicide blotters after the bound and gagged nude bodies of murder victims are found. A man in his own apartment allows a stranger to handcuff him. Once he's allowed that to happen, he is totally at the mercy of another person, about whom he knows little or nothing.

WOMEN TAKING CHANCES

Pamela Merrick, age twenty-nine, began living with her former boyfriend even though she knew he had a long record of assaults both in and out of prison. Other than some unkept promises he made to her, nothing about this guy led Pam to believe he had cooled his violent temper. But Pam took him in anyway, and it wasn't long before she regretted it.

Realizing that her old boyfriend had not changed his habits, Pam asked him to leave. Soon after, she began living with another man. As she was walking out of a downtown restaurant one night, Pam noticed her ex-boyfriend was following her. When she turned around, he punched her in the head and threatened to kill her with a knife. He said he was upset that she had kicked him out for another man. Fortunately, Pam's screams brought help, and the ex-boyfriend was scared off and arrested a short time later.

I have been seeing more and more of these cases in recent years. A woman takes up with a guy who she knows has a history of violence, then finds her life tormented. In these cases the prosecution has trouble getting a conviction because the assailant so often persuades the victim to drop all charges. He threatens that if her testimony puts him in jail, he'll come after her when he gets out. Having experienced one beating already, many women would rather forget the whole ordeal. And who can blame them. The criminal-justice system hasn't been very effective in protecting women from these types of criminals.

Pamela was fortunate that she was only beaten up. Others are not so lucky. In the rape chapter, I discussed how women risk sexual assault by bringing home someone they don't know. The risk is even greater with someone you know has a record of criminal violence.

A twenty-eight-year-old San Jose social worker recently was found nude on a bed in her apartment with a bathrobe belt tied around her neck. Her left eye was swollen and her forehead was lacerated. She had been strangled. When my detectives arrived, they found no signs of forced entry into the victim's apartment nor any indications that there had been a struggle. The crime scene told them that the victim, whom the autopsy showed to have been legally drunk, probably knew her killer.

Further investigation revealed that the woman had dated an ex-convict with a violent background who went home with her. According to some of the victim's friends, she was an outgoing, assertive woman; so, they said, she dated men who were really not compatible or suitable to her personality. In this case, the lack of good judgment, or maybe of self-esteem cost the woman her life.

7

OLDER PEOPLE . . .
COPING WITH SPECIAL FEARS

Older people in this country have become prisoners in their own homes. Many are afraid to step outside at night, others tremble when they pass a group of teenagers on the street, some won't even walk to the curb to pick up the mail.

Even though few of them will ever fall victim to serious crime, the elderly live in fear. But try telling them that their chances of being raped or beaten are actually less than a younger person's, and they won't believe it—not when the threat of crime has such a tight grip on their minds.

Although older people perceive that they are more frequent targets of criminals, which is clearly not the case, they are right about one thing: They are obviously more vulnerable targets than the rest of us. Because of their age and physical limitations, an old man or woman walking down the street at a turtle's pace poses little threat to a criminal.

Many retired persons live alone. So, when they leave their homes, no one stays behind to watch their property. Some live in central cities where crime is rampant and police services limited. Many are unable or unwilling to move out of their old inner-city neighborhoods even if they are no longer safe. Others are placed in dangerous low-rent districts by social welfare agencies.

The lifestyle led by many older persons reflects the type of crimes that are committed against them. Because many retired persons do not drive cars, for example, they have to wait for long periods at bus stops and train depots. This gives a mugger a relatively easy mark. Many senior citizens prefer to run errands at the same time every week. This lets the burglar know precisely when and how long a house will remain vacant. It also directs the con artist to the time and place where an older person will cash a social security check. And it tells the purse snatcher when the elderly are carrying large amounts of cash.

Many elderly are far too trusting of others. They were raised during an era when crime was of little concern. Today, when they invite neighborhood youths into their homes for cookies and conversation, they do not realize they may be offering a free inspection of their household valuables. In addition, the trusting nature of an older person makes him a prime candidate for the con artist.

Put all these elements together and you can see why the elderly make a perfect mark for con artists, pickpockets and burglars. That's why these three groups of criminals are responsible for the greatest number of crimes committed against older people. Yet, so often, a simple change in lifestyle would save them.

San Jose, America's fourteenth largest city, has one of the lowest crime rates in the nation. But as in many other cities, crime against the elderly is a major problem in this area. A sampling of the cases that cross my desk every day illustrates what I'm talking about:

Mary Phillips, age sixty-six, boards a bus shortly before noon on her way to do some grocery shopping. As she rides several blocks and stares out the window at passersby, Mary fails to notice the seventeen-year-old boy who got on at the same stop she did. When Mary gets off the bus, the youth suddenly grabs her purse and takes off on foot. Even though the robbery took place during the daytime in plain view of the bus driver, several passengers and a number of other bystanders, it happened so quickly that nothing could be done. Distracted, Mary didn't even get a glimpse of the kid. She was out $78 in food stamps and $20 in cash.

John Gaven, age eighty-six, has lived by himself in an affluent neighborhood since his wife died several years ago. Every morning, John eats breakfast and reads the newspaper at the same family restaurant. John always dresses well, carries at least a couple of hundred dollars with him and pays his tab in cash. One day, when John returned home, he found his house ransacked. Missing were several thousands of dollars' worth of jewelry and $250 in cash.

Glenda Joyce, eighty-five, was shopping at K-Mart for gifts for her grandchildren when she stopped to try on a pair of shoes. Other shoppers in the store told police that a woman in her mid twenties grabbed Glenda's purse from her shopping cart and ran out of the store. Poor Glenda had no idea what happened. She was too busy looking for a new pair of shoes. The thief got away with $30 cash and all of Glenda's credit cards, leaving her without money to purchase her grandkids' gifts, her shoes, without even the bus fare home.

THE MOST COMMON CRIMES

Among the most common crimes committed against the elderly are strong-arm robbery, burglary and purse snatching. According to a recent report by the U.S. Justice Department, three out of every four crimes against the elderly are common thefts—not rape, not murder, not even violent assault.

The following figures taken from a 1976 study of 180 police departments by the International Association of Chiefs of Police should open the eyes of many older persons who keep themselves locked up in their houses. The numbers represent in ranking order the percentages of various crimes that are committed against senior citizens:

• Confidence games	83%
• Purse snatching and pickpocket	72%
• Burglary	68%
• Vandalism	55%
• Theft of checks	55%
• Robbery	37%
• Telephone harassment	18%

- Threats   15%
- Auto theft   11%
- Aggravated assault   11%
- Rape   1%

These statistics should calm many older persons who are frightened about violent crimes. The elderly who are afraid to leave their homes during the day are not worried so much about con artists, pickpockets and vandals as they are about vicious killers and rapists. But it is a rare occasion when old people are attacked by violent criminals. The same is true of sexual assault. Most rape victims are young women, not old ladies.

It's no secret that crime is more traumatic to the elderly. Younger people are employed and more likely to be able to recoup financial losses, while many retired persons on fixed incomes are financially and emotionally devastated by similar events. Young and middle-aged adults recover from broken bones and injuries much faster than do senior citizens. So, although the crime rate against seniors is much lower, the physical and emotional disruption is greater.

Like most police administrators, I learn a lot about the patterns of street criminals from my department's undercover decoy operations. Typically, an officer dresses up like a bum and takes a bottle of cheap wine, a roll of cash and a police transmitter and slumps in a doorway in a high-robbery area. When a robber strikes what appears to be the easiest of marks, the undercover cop moves, and so do the several other cops waiting and watching from nearby positions. Nine times out of ten, the robber is arrested and successfully prosecuted. That's because the whole episode is recorded on sound tape, and neither the victim nor the witnesses are afraid to testify—they're all cops.

Over the years, my department has found it rather easy to make cops look like winos. These undercover operations usually take place during dusk and darkness when it is much harder for a robber to distinguish between a decoy and the real thing. But when we wanted to put a stop to a series of strong-arm robberies against senior citizens, we had a problem. The robberies were taking place during the day, which meant the disguises would have to pass the intense scrutiny of pickpockets. Since most of our police personnel do not resemble the elderly—the department mostly consists of young people in their twenties and thirties—we had trouble until we contacted a couple of professional theater groups to help with the makeup job. A few hours later, a thirty-five-year-old policewoman was made up to resemble a seventy-eight-year-old lady, and we had our first arrest for purse snatching.

TRY NOT TO WALK ALONE

After making several similar arrests over a period of a week, we learned that thieves look for senior citizens who walk alone on the streets. Rarely did we find a robber who tried to strike a decoy when he or she was accompanied by someone else. These robbers, who were primarily in their teens, often struck in broad daylight. It was also apparent that they were less likely to rob a decoy who held a purse close to her body rather than loosely in her arms.

We could see that our geriatric decoy unit was much more successful on certain days than others. After a few weeks, a pattern became evident—thieves came out in droves on the first and fifteenth of the month, when the elderly received their social security, pension and welfare checks in the mail. We ran into one group of thieves that actually waited outside a bank building for old folks to cash their checks before they robbed them. In most major cities, you can accurately predict which parts of town will be purse-snatchers' havens—alleyways, bus stops, around banks and downtown streets.

Our decoy unit's experience on the streets taught us a lot about defending older people. Most crimes against the elderly are opportunistic, which means that senior citizens can take steps to significantly reduce their chances of becoming victims. The most obvious piece of advice is not to walk alone on the streets. Elderly persons should always arrange to shop in groups.

If you must go out alone, be certain to walk near groups of people. Also, older persons should have their checks deposited automatically, carry only small amounts of cash and leave their purses at home. If a purse must be taken along, it should be kept as close to the body as possible, with one arm around it. Never wrap the strap around your wrist or arm because if the purse is snatched, you could get pulled to the ground.

VARY YOUR ROUTINE

Most older persons don't realize that they actually have an advantage over other age groups when it comes to protecting themselves. Most of us leave our homes each day to work an eight-hour shift. Nothing could be more comforting to a burglar. Retired people, on the other hand, have much more flexibility and are not tied to such a rigid schedule. They can arrange bank visits, grocery shopping and errands at safe times, or maybe even postpone such trips until a son, daughter, neighbor or friend can accompany them.

The unfortunate thing is that so many senior citizens do not arrange their schedules to minimize potential dangers. Many, for instance, insist on being very orderly and prefer doing their grocery shopping on the same day week after week. While maintaining such a schedule may be convenient for a retiree, even psychologically comforting, it's foolish as far as crime prevention goes. Such a consistent pattern assists the criminal in mapping his crimes in advance.

Here are some other tips for older persons:

1. Criminals often prey on seniors who look confused or passive. If you must walk by yourself, be alert and confident. Know where you are going and be aware of other people in front of and behind you. If you suspect someone is following you, head for an open business. Even though you might not know a store clerk, they are usually

very helpful when it comes to assisting the elderly under such circumstances.

2. The streets are the most common spot for a senior to become a crime victim. If you use public transit, sit close to the driver and place your packages between yourself and the window. When walking to or from your residence, stay in the center of the sidewalk. When shopping, walk with groups of people to and from the store. Before entering your car, check the rear seat to see if anyone is hiding there. Do not keep car doors open when arranging packages or adjusting seat belts, because you're just giving the purse snatcher more time to complete his mission.

3. You will be less vulnerable to thieves if you don't carry large sums of cash. Use checks, credit cards or money orders instead of cash when you can. You can recover credit cards and cancel them when they are lost, but you can't recover cash. Avoid unnecessary trips to your bank branch, especially around social security payment days and Fridays (payday), when crooks are on the lookout for victims. Instead, deposit your checks directly by mail.

4. The average victim of purse snatching is over fifty-five; the average suspect is under twenty-four. So avoid areas where youths congregate, especially school grounds. Keep your distance from kids who ride city buses and hang out at bus stops. Your best bet is to stay near groups of adults. Ask your local police department to pay special attention to teenage gangs and to send an officer to functions where seniors have to use public transportation. Representatives from a local senior citizens' group or the regional association of retired persons organization can be helpful with these requests.

5. If you are attacked, sit down right away to avoid being pushed to the ground and injured. Carry a whistle you can blow to attract attention. I recommend carrying a portable siren. Do not resist purse snatchers. They usually are excited and may be easily provoked. Take a good look at the suspect and note any details that will help

you describe him. When trying to determine age, height, weight and appearance, compare the attacker to other people you know or even to yourself. Memorize peculiarities such as tattoos, marks and scars or other prominent physical features. Note the direction taken by your attacker and, if possible, write down a license number and vehicle description if a car is involved.

6. Your cooperation in working with the police will go a long way in catching your attacker. Telephone the police department right away. There is no time for delay. Tell the police dispatcher you have been robbed and answer his questions quickly and calmly. The police can work only on the information you give them, so be accurate. When the call comes in, the robbery is broadcast to all police units on duty. If the officers have pertinent information a few minutes after a robbery, the chances of capturing the suspect increase greatly. Don't be reluctant or afraid to cooperate with detectives by making yourself available for interviews and police lineups.

8
PROTECTING YOUR KIDS

Every parent is concerned about the safety of his or her children. Mostly we worry when they stay out late at night, or aren't home in time for dinner. When our kids are at school or home, however, we are often lulled into a false sense of security by thinking they are protected.

Many parents aren't aware that school and home are the two places where our children are most often raped, robbed and beaten. In fact, a majority of crimes committed against youths away from home occur on school grounds. A federal study of twenty-six American cities found that 8 percent of all the crimes in the United States took place on school campuses. Many of the crimes were petty thefts and assaults that resulted in minor injuries.

"Survival in school once meant merely passing examinations," U.S. Congressman Mario Biaggi of New York observed, at a 1978 Congressional committee hearing on school safety. (Biaggi is a former NYPD cop who was broken in many years ago by my father, then a beat cop.) "Today, survival in many American schools means escaping from the thousands of criminals who roam hallways and playgrounds with unrestricted ease and terrorize students and teachers alike."

During a recent period of fifty-eight school days, officials in one California school district collected 88 guns and 243 knives from various campuses. More than 105,000 incidents of violence or vandalism were reported in California schools during one semester. That is only the tip of the iceberg. A majority of school crimes are never reported to authorities.

Two dozen California public-school teachers are assaulted every day (usually by their students), and an average of 215 students are attacked daily on school grounds. The problem became so severe that in 1980 then Attorney General George Deukmejian filed a lawsuit against the Los Angeles School District and the LAPD to force them to protect school-children.

I think many children live in terror during the time they spend in school. They probably don't talk about it much, but deep down they are afraid of being attacked or having their belongings stolen. In fact, a 1978 federal study found that nine of every ten students and three of every four teachers who were victims of rape, robbery and aggravated assault on school grounds did not report crimes to police. Parents should demand to know what school and police officials are doing to protect their children during school hours. I have long believed that school authorities report only a fraction of crimes to police because they are afraid of rocking the boat. For the same reasons, many school officials have failed to react to the crime wave that has hit our schools. These people need to be made aware of just how serious the problem is.

Here is some advice for parents on what they can do about school violence.

1. Make sure that your children feel free to talk to you about anything that might happen to them at school.
2. Visit your children's school yourself to see if you observe any people hanging around with no apparent business near schools or playgrounds.
3. Alert your children to stay away from strangers, and inform them of the tricks that child molesters frequently use.
4. Encourage your youngsters to feel free to seek help from police officers, teachers and neighbors if they are being followed by strangers.
5. Teenagers should stay clear of youth gangs in schools.

I've already indicated that your home isn't a very safe place unless you've taken some of the basic precautions suggested in this book. This is particularly true for children who stay home by themselves after school. Remember the rape chapter and the young girls who were assaulted in their own bedrooms after school? If your home is lacking adequate safeguards, your child could easily become the next victim.

Crimes committed against children by family members are a whole different category. Such offenses as child abuse and molestation are rarely reported to police. As you will see, these crimes are among the most devastating committed against children.

The home is one of the places where children are most likely to be molested or abused. Only in recent years has our society begun to realize the magnitude of this problem. Police, school authorities, emergency-room doctors and nurses are far more likely to recognize and report child abuse now than a few years ago. Similarly, parents need to understand that other people who visit their home—relatives, neighbors, friends—may pose a danger to their children. For example, children from a woman's previous marriage often are sexually molested by a new boyfriend or husband. Police receive many child-abuse reports that point to a favorite uncle or grandparent.

TALK OPENLY WITH YOUR KIDS

The first precaution parents must take is to play straight with their children. Tell your kids that if anyone ever asks them to disrobe, takes off his or her own clothes or tries to touch parts of their bodies, they should tell you immediately. The only cases that police can investigate are the ones we know of. Child abusers are very successful at using threats to prevent their victims from telling on them, and most kids don't tell their parents out of confused fear that *they* have done something wrong.

Because they are in a position to take advantage of children when no one is around, baby-sitters are often implicated in cases of child molestation. I am always shocked at how many parents entrust the lives and safety of their children to young people they know so little about.

The case of ten-week-old Travis Coleman is one tragic example. The little boy's mother left him with a nineteen-year-old baby-sitter who had had four children mysteriously die while in her care. Travis became the fifth. The mother, seventeen, said she had heard some talk about the baby-sitter in her small Florida town, but she didn't believe it. The sitter's background speaks for itself: As a youth she was tossed back and forth from home to home by relatives and social workers. She had a juvenile criminal record that went back six years. At the time of the deaths, she faced six bad-check charges. After three days in the eighth grade, she left school to get married. The marriage ended six weeks later. She tried to have children twice but both attempts ended with miscarriages. At age sixteen, she attempted suicide.

In defense of the mother of Travis Coleman, she had no idea that the baby-sitter was to blame for the four prior deaths. Neither did legal authorities, at the time. It was not until baby Travis died that authorities became suspicious and the baby-sitter was arrested. She eventually confessed to the killings—all stranglings—and was convicted on two counts of murder.

Unfortunately, the mother of little Travis Coleman reacted like many parents—she chose to ignore details, such as the juvenile criminal record, that would have convinced her to look for another sitter. That mother's oversight is by no means unusual.

A San Jose couple recently hired a nineteen-year-old boy to watch their seven-year-old daughter. A couple of days later, the little girl told her mom that the sitter had taken her clothes off and laid on top of her. The parents were shocked. It had not even occurred to them to check out the sitter's background beforehand.

In another case, a young mother dropped off her eight-year-old daughter at a San Jose day-care center that she knew very little about. Later that night, the little girl told her mother that a man employed by the center had undressed her and put his penis in her mouth.

CHECK OUT BABY-SITTERS, DAY-CARE CENTERS

It is so easy to reduce the number of sexual abuses of children by investigating the background of a baby-sitter or a day-care center. Yet it usually takes a tragic incident for many parents to do so. The simplest way is to seek recommendations and character references from neighbors and friends. When you hire a baby-sitter, think of that person as a job applicant. Most employers don't hire strangers off the street. Neither should you. If there is some reason to question a person's background, don't give him the benefit of the doubt as Travis Coleman's mother did. Contact the police, school officials and local or state child-care licensing facilities to assist your background search.

Once you have checked out a prospective baby-sitter, don't stop there. Make sure that your child has a phone number of a neighbor or relative in case something happens. And don't hesitate to pay the sitter an unannounced visit to make sure everything is okay.

STRANGERS

When it comes to strangers, most parents realize the need to caution their children. A San Jose case that attracted nationwide attention shows what can happen to children who are not extremely suspicious of people they don't know. It involved a twelve-year-old girl who was kidnapped one afternoon as she walked home from school. The girl was held captive for five months, in a pit with dirt walls, before she was released. The

117

kidnapper eventually pleaded guilty to six counts of child abuse and was sentenced to twenty-five years in prison.

What is to be learned from such cases? Again, parents must be open with their kids and tell them that there are bad people in the world who harm children. Be sure to instruct them to run for help at the first sign of trouble when a stranger approaches. As painful as it might be for all parents, there comes a time when we must shatter our youngsters' innocence and warn them about evil people. Most good police departments have extensive education programs for elementary students, called "Officer Bill" or "Officer Friendly." They are aimed at teaching children to be suspicious of strangers and to avoid contact with them.

Some parents sneer at the oft-repeated advice to children— don't accept any gifts or go for a ride with strangers. Yet every year thousands of young children are molested, assaulted and some even killed when they fall for the old approach of offering candy as a lure. Some sex criminals have an uncanny ability to disarm children's suspicions. Even bright youngsters who have been warned by their parents can momentarily succumb to the appeal of petting a kitten or eating an ice-cream cone. It seems that no matter how many times we warn children not to take gifts or candy from strangers, they continue to be fooled by them. Kids who are particularly obedient may be told by the molester that their parents have been hurt. He then offers to take the child home.

"FRIENDS"

Sometimes it's the people kids trust the most whom parents need to be concerned about. A number of community leaders, such as Little League coaches, scoutmasters, teachers and priests, have been found guilty of molesting children.

In St. Petersburg, Florida, a forty-two-year-old scoutmaster was recently sent to prison for fifteen years after pleading guilty to molesting young scouts on camping trips. Some of the boys submitted to the scout leader's wishes so they could get ahead in their troop. Others, according to the prosecutor in the case, consented because they were afraid of getting hurt.

In Fremont, California, a seventy-year-old Catholic monsignor resigned from his church amid accusations that he sexually abused young girls. A police investigation found that the priest fondled eight girls between seven and fourteen when they visited the church rectory. The monsignor was not charged with any criminal wrongdoing; but under a compromise worked out by the church, he was forced to resign, receive psychiatric counseling and be reassigned to an area where he would not come in contact with children.

While these cases obviously do not reflect on the kind of people who volunteer to become scout leaders or enter the priesthood, they do show a need for parents to keep informed of their children's activities. Both investigations began when the young victims brought the abuses to the attention of parents. More often, kids who are victimized by adults do not speak up.

DICKIE WAVERS

Parents also must beware of exhibitionists who get a thrill out of exposing themselves to young children. Better known as "dickie wavers" in police jargon, these people are usually mentally disturbed and often have a record of prior arrests and convictions, which they serve in facilities for sex offenders. Recently, I asked my sex-crimes unit to provide me with a log of all cases against children. What I found was consistent with what I have long known to be the case—these exhibitionists are everywhere. Here are some cases in just a one-month period:

Susie, age eleven, and a friend were on a school playground swing when a man ran by, pulled down his shorts and masturbated in front of them.

Karen, age thirteen, was riding home from school on a city bus when a man seated next to her took out his penis and began stroking it.

119

Janet, age eleven, told her mother that whenever she and her friends play in front of their apartment complex, a man undresses and stands nude in front of his nearby bedroom window.

Lisa, age nine, looked up from the dice game she was playing with her friends to observe a man drive up in a vehicle and open the door. He was wearing only a T-shirt.

These incidents never make headlines in the newspaper, but they happen all the time. Ask any big-city police department. Most dickie wavers are not violent, but they do cause psychological trauma for many little kids. Some of these exhibitionists also "graduate" to more violent behavior and become rapists. For this reason, parents, school authorities and police all need to pay special attention to strangers who loiter around school grounds for no apparent reason.

The best advice you can give your children is to immediately report such conduct to school authorities. In turn, the prompt reporting to police enables us to check these characters out and quickly determine if they have any kind of criminal history of sex-related offenses.

9
BEATING THE BURGLARS

You're driving back from a weekend vacation when suddenly you remember that you forgot to leave a light on at home. As you pull into the darkness of the driveway, you hope no one broke into your place while you were away. You take a deep breath, unlock the door and find everything inside in order.

If you've ever had that feeling, you're not alone. Millions of Americans live in fear of getting ripped off. Whether you own a house, live in a condominium or rent an apartment, you have every reason to worry about burglars. Each year, they break into nearly 5 million residences.

Despite these figures, many folks don't bother to adequately safeguard their homes. They believe with some justification that a burglar will break in if he wants, regardless of the security precautions taken. You can hardly blame them for feeling as they do. How many times have you heard or read about big-time thieves overcoming "burglarproof" systems to steal valuable jewels.

One such criminal was "The Cat." He only hit the best pads in Los Angeles. For three years he prowled the posh streets of Beverly Hills, pulling some 150 burglaries. At least that's all he confessed to. Police believe that The Cat, who started his career at age nineteen, was responsible for many more. The Cat was not your run-of-the-mill house thief. He never messed around with an estate valued at less than a quarter-million bucks. Nor did he take heavy items such as furniture, stereos or TV sets. The Cat's market was strictly cash and jewels. Sometimes he used sophisticated tools to get past locks and burglar alarms. Mostly, though, his clients left doors open for him.

The Cat never conducted business when people were home. He knocked on doors and broke in when no one answered. The Cat didn't have to knock on many doors before he found an empty house. Perhaps that's because rich folks in Beverly Hills like to eat out and party a lot. The Cat was eventually collared by police on routine patrol. Detectives estimated he made off with hundreds of thousands of dollars in stolen goods. He's free now after spending eight months behind bars.

What can you do, other than pray, to prevent someone like The Cat from picking on your place? Nothing, really. Nonetheless, most of us will never have to worry about the professional burglar, like The Cat. I don't want to hurt your feelings, but a pro is not interested in you unless your name is Vanderbilt or something like it. The top-notch thief is too snobbish to even consider anything but the highest return on his investment. Why should he risk himself and waste his valuable time on poor folks?

If you're like me and wonder how you're going to put the kids through college, you don't have to worry about the pros, but you should be concerned about the run-of-the-mill burglar. I call him the opportunist. He's not very smart nor does he do his homework. He simply takes advantage of the many people who leave doors unlocked and windows open. Anything you can do to protect your home from the opportunist makes his work that much more difficult.

While the skilled burglar will always get inside a house if he is determined, the opportunist is not so sophisticated in his planning. Tight security on your part will go a long way in persuading the average burglar to prey on a careless neighbor whose place offers easier pickings.

Burglars vary in age, sex, skill and lifestyle. And if you think they are all drug addicts, forget it. While the proceeds of knocking over your house may well purchase some drugs on the black market, they may also go toward paying for college tuition, flashy cars and fancy clothes.

Unfortunately, cops don't catch many burglars. Less than one in every five gets arrested. There are so many burglaries nowadays that most major police departments are unable to attend to most of them. In 1981, for example, only 15 percent of San Jose's nearly 15,000 burglaries were actually investigated. The reports were taken over the phone and filed for insurance purposes. The reason for the lack of attention is really quite simple: most burglaries have little or no chance of getting solved. Unless a burglary victim is able to furnish police with concrete leads, such as a vehicle description, a fingerprint or other physical evidence, the detectives are just wasting their time.

From the few burglars who do get arrested, I know that an overwhelming majority are men, and half are under seventeen. Eighty percent have some kind of criminal record, and many are caught within a mile of their home. Most burglars are after items that will bring them quick cash. Some even steal on order. The goods that usually bring the most money are jewelry, firearms, TV sets and stereos.

While "robbery" may mean the same thing as "burglary" to many people, there is a big difference between them. You rob people, not houses. A robbery is when someone forcibly takes an item away from a person, as in a street mugging, for example, or when a robber takes money at gunpoint from a bank teller. When someone walks into a store and takes merchandise, that is theft. Burglary, according to the FBI, is when someone unlawfully enters a building to commit a felony or theft. However, you can commit a residential burglary without ever breaking into a house. It is still considered a burglary when a stranger walks into your open garage and takes a bicycle.

DON'T ATTRACT TROUBLE

The first thing you should know about burglars is that your lifestyle could lead one to your house. Consider the person who flashes a wad of bills at the corner store to pay for a six-pack of beer. Or, a man who tries to impress his date by giving a kid a $10 tip for washing his Porsche. These incidents may appear trivial to you, but they could easily lead the store clerk or car-wash employee to believe that you've got money. If a burglar believes you are wealthy and breaks into your place, he might be disappointed to find that you're not that well off. But by then it's too late, and he'll walk off with whatever you have.

The person who has an occasional party where drugs are provided also runs the risk of setting himself up as a potential target for burglars. The host usually isn't aware that by associating with a friend or co-worker who has drug connections, he has placed one foot into the underworld. When these characters and their friends show up at the party, they get a free inspection tour of the host's valuables and his home-security system. When the house is hit sometime later, the homeowner has no inkling that the party and the burglary are related.

Burglary is a $3.3-billion-a-year industry. The average take is $882 per house—not bad for a few minutes' work. The worst thing about burglary is that it is a highly personal crime. Victims rarely suffer physical injuries but are often emotionally affected when their privacy has been invaded—they find beds overturned, drawers emptied, furniture destroyed and windows broken. Long after the burglar is gone and the house cleaned up, the effect lingers. Many victims don't feel safe sleeping in their houses until the burglar is caught. Others fear the burglar has taken a set of house keys and will return at a later date. Some never recover from the loss of a family heirloom or a special piece of jewelry. While such items have little monetary value to the burglar, they are priceless to the owner.

One clear pattern emerges: While violent crimes frequently take place at night and on weekends, the majority of burglaries occur during the day. A burglar's schedule is planned around your work hours. The last thing he wants is to be confronted while he is cleaning out a house.

Before you go about protecting your house or apartment against burglars, you need to determine who the enemy is.

THE PROFESSIONAL

Perhaps the most prolific specialist in the world of crime, the professional burglar is a special breed of criminal. He wouldn't steal your Mercedes-Benz, even if you left the garage door wide open and the keys in the ignition. That's because the professional doesn't go on fishing expeditions. He does not pull a job without knowing what to expect. He carefully studies the potential worth of a prospective victim and devises plans to overcome alarm systems and Doberman pinschers. As noted, the professional generally won't waste his time unless his research indicates you are wealthy. If you are not but still might have, say, a Picasso hanging on a living-room wall, or an expensive sculpture in the foyer, your house could be in jeopardy.

Wellington P. Cheng knows the type of place that professional burglars choose to enter. Cheng is a Taiwanese businessman whose posh Bel Air estate in Los Angeles was burglarized last year. He lost nearly $5 million worth of jewels, art and cash. The thieves bypassed a sophisticated alarm system and a number of exterior floodlights to load a truck full of grandfather clocks, 300-pound statues, and jewels valued at $1.75 million.

The professional often works with inside information gathered from a network of reliable sources. These tips provide him with advance knowledge of the kind of goods he can expect to steal. They come from a variety of people—milkmen, servants, house guests, garbage collectors, and even neighborhood kids who do odd jobs.

One such person, for example, may be an attendant who works at a parking garage. Besides parking cars, he might also check out customers who leave the keys to their expensive automobiles in his not-so-trustworthy hands. Once he finds a wealthy candidate who is spending a night on the town, the attendant goes to work laying the foundation for a major burglary. First, he makes a wax impression of the customer's house key for later duplication. Next, he opens the glove box to get an address from the vehicle registration. Once the job is finished at his end, the real experts take over and stake out the house. If the estate is an acceptable "hit"—in other words, if the customer has enough worth stealing—the burglary is pulled off with relative ease. For his efforts, the cooperative garage attendant gets a slice of the take.

When the professional isn't hooking up with his sources, he lets his "fingers do the walking," not through the Yellow Pages but in journals that list the nation's wealthiest individuals. In Greenwich, Connecticut, police recently noticed a peculiar pattern to a string of big-time burglaries—most of the victims' addresses were listed in the *Social Register*, a guide to America's most prominent families. About 400 of the 50,000 named in the *Register* reside in Greenwich, home for a number of Manhattan's wealthiest business people. In many of the break-ins, the burglars slipped past fancy alarms to take thousands of dollars' worth of property. When police stopped three men suspected of committing the burglaries, they found two copies of the *Register* in their car. A detective noticed check marks next to the names of persons whose homes had been burglarized. The burglars had used the *Register* as their own personal guide to some of the best targets in America.

Once the professional selects his victim, he breaks in using a variety of methods. Some specialize in roof entries. Others rely on deactivating intricate alarm systems. Many are good locksmiths. You can buy the best locks in the world but they won't stop a burglar who has a wide range of lock-picking tools at his disposal. The pro doesn't mess around with crude devices such as crowbars. Rather, he quietly goes about using the latest and most sophisticated tools available to the locksmith trade.

If, however, the professional thinks a house is burglarproof—and few are—he is smart enough to move on to another prospective target. A handful of professional burglars regard the best-secured homes as the greatest challenges. The few pros who do get caught are usually nailed because they bit off more than they could chew.

One such case involved the art-rug burglar. At age thirty-nine he was a track coach, art connoisseur and father of four. Police think he took as much as $3 million in property over a two-year period in a spectacular series of 130 break-ins on the Peninsula, a ritzy area in northern California that is home to Silicon Valley executives and Stanford University professors. The art-rug burglar had all the credentials of a professional. He crawled through incredibly small windows to silently remove the finest treasures. Once, he picked the six rarest bottles of French wine from a cabinet holding about twenty vintages. He also took an authentic painting off one wall and left a reproduction undisturbed. He was a superb athlete who twice eluded police on foot. He even pulled off a few burglaries in neighborhoods that were staked out by police.

As it turned out, the art-rug burglar underwent an excellent training program to become a top-notch thief. He served a year in a California prison camp in 1973 for possessing stolen property, and two more years in state prison on burglary charges. Despite his success, the art-rug burglar was captured because he made too many little mistakes. For instance, any professional knows that he ought to dispose of stolen property quickly so he is not caught with the evidence. But the art-rug burglar kept an inventory of stolen goods in his house and two storage lockers full of various items that it would have taken years to fence. A raid of his house turned up $750,000 worth of stolen property that included guns, diamonds, cameras, lush Oriental rugs and silver. Police carted off another $750,000 worth from the storage lockers.

The art-rug burglar apparently never worried about getting caught, a weakness that led to his eventual downfall. When he consigned stolen goods to an art dealer, using his own name, police had the lead that would eventually send them to his doorstep. Worse yet, the art-rug burglar didn't even bother to hide much of what he took. He repainted a stolen van in his driveway, used stolen cameras in his free-lance photography business, put stolen rugs on his floors, placed stolen china in a cabinet, and kept stolen precious gems on hand. While most professionals go for stuff they can unload within an hour, the art-rug burglar picked up items for his family—a bottle of Chanel No. 5, an Abyssinian cat, a can of baked beans, a Snoopy wristwatch, a cockatoo, Nike jackets and Adidas running shoes. He even gave stolen cameras, coins and silver jewelry to the young students on his track team. During the police raid, detectives took a stolen jacket off the back of one of the art-rug burglar's sons.

THE SEMIPROFESSIONAL

If you're like me, you don't have thousands of dollars in jewels, silver and cash lying around the house to attract the professional burglar. Probably the most sophisticated thief you need to worry about is the semiprofessional. For him burglary is an easy way to acquire property. He knows that few burglars are caught and even fewer go to jail. That's why, even though he lacks the expertise of a professional, the semiprofessional can still earn a good living.

Often the semiprofessional is in business to support a drug habit, rather than a wife and kids. Or he is a career criminal who has spent several years in prison. Sometimes bad luck will do him in—someone happens to interrupt a burglary or a squad car drives by at the wrong time. Or, as is more often the case, the semiprofessional is double-crossed by an angry girlfriend or partner who goes to the police.

Just because the semiprofessional successfully pulls off a string of burglaries without ever getting caught doesn't mean he is a genius. Far from it. He just takes advantage of easy marks, such as apartments, motels and middle-class neighborhoods. He is willing to take a small risk without being exactly sure what he'll find inside. His goals are far more modest than those of the professional. Indeed, the semiprofessional would not even recognize an original Picasso.

The semiprofessional relies on some rather unsophisticated techniques in casing a house. Two incidents that occurred recently in my neighborhood provide good examples. The first time, I was leaving for work when a man came to the front door to ask for help. He said his car was stalled in a park around the corner, and he wanted to know if I could give him a jump start. What a complete stranger was doing in my neighborhood park early on a weekday morning puzzled me. So I suggested he call a garage. When I had my people check his license number, they learned he was a paroled burglar. He was going door to door, asking for help. When no one answered, he had himself an unoccupied home. In this case, all the police could do was stop him for questioning and put him out of work for a day.

The second time, I was jogging through the same park when I spotted two scurvy-looking characters eyeing a nearby house. I called the department, and within five minutes these two gentlemen were being questioned by two of my police officers. The men said they were enjoying some fresh air in the park. The cops ran their names through the computer and found that both men were burglars on parole.

You may take offense at my seemingly automatic assumption of the guilt of ex-convicts who appear to be minding their own business. But the fact is that six of every ten burglars on the street today have spent time in prison. And nearly half are actually on parole or probation at the time they are caught. While I'm not advocating that you assume everyone who has a burglary record will commit another offense, these figures ought to make you suspicious.

The Semipro's Inside View

Some semiprofessional burglars work in legitimate jobs. They might be painters, rug installers, drivers, postal employees or even police officers. They are usually people whose work offers them an inside edge on stealing property. Take a realtor. Each week he has special access to hundreds of homes listed for sale. He can show a piece of property to an interested buyer by taking a house key from a hidden metal lockbox. Many realtors have used these lockbox keys to enter homes alone and remove valuable items. They take great care not to ransack a house so the owners do not become aware that something is missing until after they move. Then the homeowner will blame himself for misplacing an item rather than suspect the professional realtor.

One of the most sensational lockbox cases in California was that of the "Tippy-toe" burglar. Before she began this kind of theft, Tippy-toe gained prominence in the early 1960s for prowling bachelors' apartments in San Jose. When she found an unlocked door late at night, she tiptoed into a bedroom, grabbed a wallet and ran. Few men chased after her, usually because of their state of undress. Before she was caught and sentenced to prison, Tippy-toe was living the "good life." She had a chauffeur, a maid, elegant clothes and maintained a $100-a-day heroin habit.

After serving three years in state prison, Tippy-toe was released and became director of a San Jose drug recovery center. She had done such a good job of rehabilitating herself that Governor Edmund G. Brown, Jr., pardoned her in 1981. The pardon allowed Tippy-toe to retain all her civil and political rights. But not for long. Six months later, the forty-seven-year-old woman was arrested on fifteen counts of burglary and possession of stolen property. Within a three-month period she had received her real estate license and begun burglarizing houses with keys taken from lockboxes. When police searched her home, they recovered about 300 items, including bracelets, earrings, coin collections, watches, diamond rings and revolvers. Many of Tippy-toe's victims never realized something valuable was missing

Although Tippy-toe pulled off each crime by herself, many semiprofessionals operate in groups. Unfortunately, this goes for some police officers, too. Recently, at least ten cops in the Hollywood division of the Los Angeles Police Department were implicated in an extensive burglary ring. Whenever the cops were dispatched to the scene of a burglary, they checked the premises to make sure no suspects were around. Then, before they contacted the police station, the cops helped themselves to cash, video cassette recorders, tapes of their favorite movies—anything the original burglars left behind. After they stashed the stuff in the trunks of their squad cars, the police informed the victims of the break-in. At one point the practice was so widespread that different cops on the same force were racing each other to the scene of burglaries.

You can help deter the burglar by recording serial numbers and marking all your valuables. Most people don't bother, which partly explains why only 2 percent of all stolen property recovered in this country is returned. One of the most frustrating aspects of police work is to recover thousands of valuable items from a major burglary sting only to see the stuff sit around in some warehouse because the owners could not prove the merchandise was theirs. It happens all the time.

Stinging Semipros

Police often nab semiprofessional burglars by conducting undercover sting operations. It is rare for a cop on routine patrol to run into a burglary ring. To complicate matters, most residents don't discover that a burglary has taken place until after the thief is gone. That leaves the sting as the one effective weapon to catch career burglars.

The San Jose Police Department recently put three undercover cops in street clothes in a downtown furniture store as part of an undercover sting. We let word out in various bars, pool halls and other places where thieves congregate that the furniture store was buying stolen property. At first, burglars trickled in slowly to exchange their hot goods for cold cash. As word spread that the store was offering a reasonable exchange rate, the place became a supermarket for stolen property. The burglars, who brought in a wide variety of merchandise, were impressed with the hospitality of the men who ran the furniture-store operation. For instance, the undercover cops always offered their clients a cold beer. But the burglars never realized that as they negotiated the price of stolen tools, handguns, TV sets, silverware, etc., the entire transaction was recorded by a camera hidden in a wall. The opening of the refrigerator that contained the beer automatically started the camera.

About half of the people caught on film were on parole or

probation for a prior theft. A good many had been sent to local rehabilitation programs that apparently failed to do the job. Some of the burglars actually bragged on camera to the undercover cops about their past. They were proud of their bank robberies and long prison sentences. One guy went so far as to offer to carry out a murder for $500. He said that a broken arm or leg would cost a nominal fee. A check of the guy's record revealed that he had once been arrested for murder and had done time for bank robbery.

What emerged on camera was a group of people who regard you and me as a means for them to avoid ever having to work for a living. They are confident they can commit hundreds of burglaries without ever getting convicted.

The undercover operation was a smashing success. Trusting burglars sold us everything from stereos and home computers to machine guns, all of which was booked as evidence. In all, 150 burglars were caught fencing more than one million dollars in property. We nabbed three youngsters between the ages of sixteen and twenty-two who were specialists at stealing computer and office equipment from new electronics firms. These kids were hitting so frequently that they brought in $200,000 in stolen goods. To discourage them, the undercover cops finally said they couldn't take any more. This didn't help; the threesome phoned back the next night from inside another company—their sixth burglary in one day—to say they had a stack of typewriters and a dilemma. Two vehicles were in the building, a truck and a Cadillac. Which one did the cops want? They said neither, but the youths showed up outside the furniture store anyway with the truck full of typewriters.

Another group of semiprofessionals was so successful that they visited our furniture shop practically every other day. They worked at residential burglaries like factory workers on an assembly line. Their productivity gave us a real headache. We couldn't stand by idly and let these burglars continue to rip off the city at such a frantic pace. On the other hand, once you arrest a suspect, the sting's whole cover blows up in your face. A burglary sting has to run for nearly a year in most U.S. cities to become cost effective in terms of the number of arrests made and the amount of property recovered. So we didn't know quite what to do about this very industrious group. Fortunately for us, one of the burglars told the undercover cops a great deal about how they ripped people off. The information was relayed to street officers who patrolled the neighborhoods where these burglars worked, and who later arrested them for possession of stolen property. To this day, the burglars have no idea that the undercover cops at the downtown furniture store and the uniformed cops who arrested them worked together.

THE OPPORTUNIST

This is the thief you need to worry about most. He is your run-of-the-mill everyday burglar, usually a teenage truant who takes your property during the day while his classmates are in school studying and you are away working. I call the average burglar "the opportunist" because he is not so much a sophisticated crook as a delinquent who takes what is given him. The opportunist is smart enough not to attempt to break into a well-secured house or apartment. But he will seize upon the opportunity to burglarize when someone has failed to lock a door or window. Such carelessness makes the opportunist's job a snap.

The main difference between the opportunist and semipro is that the opportunist is likely to be a less-skilled teenager. Sometimes the defenses taken against the opportunist are not adequate for the semipro. For example, an empty alarm box probably wouldn't be as likely to fool the semipro as it would the opportunist. Similarly, the opportunist who sees a charli bar in a sliding glass door will give up and go off with his teenage buddies to drink beer or play basketball in the park. The semipro will go on to pry open your back door or a window.

If a middle-class neighborhood is hit by a rash of burglaries, chances are the residents know the burglar. In fact, they may know the burglar so well, they would never suspect him of any wrongdoing. He probably is a teenager who lives nearby, struggling in school, with no job. Often, the first time such an opportunist hits a house, he did not even plan the crime. But when he sees several newspapers stacked on a neighbor's doorstep, the temptation is too great. And once he realizes how easy it is to earn big money for so little effort, he begins hitting the other neighbors. I have seen this pattern over and over again.

Even a police chief is not immune to the opportunist. Recently, while my wife and I were in Atlanta for the annual convention of the International Association of Chiefs of Police, three neighborhood teenagers tried to break into my home. One of them had learned from a friend of my teenage daughter that we were out of town for the week. Ironically, I was conducting a hearing on crime prevention when I received a message to call my seventeen-year-old son. He had come home from school during lunch and heard a knock. Before he could open the door he heard a voice near the side of the house say, "Give me a boost." My son did exactly what we instruct all our children to do in such a situation—he called the police emergency number. About thirty seconds later a startled police dispatcher called back and asked, "Isn't this Chief McNamara's house?" My son assured the dispatcher that it was, and within minutes a police unit arrived at the house. Meanwhile, the youths had climbed onto the roof to break in through the skylight. But when they heard my son answer the phone, they fled in a car.

Fortunately, an attentive neighbor noticed the three teens running from my house and got their license-plate number. A short while later the police captured the youths outside their parents' house two blocks away. My neighbor had attended home-alert meetings in the past and told me he had become suspicious when the youths left in such a hurry. His actions are proof that neighbors working together are their own best defenders against crime.

In this case, had the youths attempted to break in they would have encountered some surprises along the way. For now, that's all I'll explain about the security measures in my house, since my family still lives there. Anyway, an adequate alarm system and alert neighbors are enough to discourage burglars such as these three kids. Remember, the opportunist is easily deterred. He doesn't carry maps of your house or stake out a residence for hours before breaking in. He simply takes what he can get and usually what comes his way. If your home has good locks, a barking dog or an alarm system, the opportunist will likely try somewhere else.

Obviously, the opportunist has little expertise or training. He crawls around your house checking doorknobs and windows. You'd be surprised how often he goes no further than to push a window open. If there are no easy entry points, he looks for a fragile garage door, a loose window or a weak latch. All it takes is a stiff shoulder and he's in business.

Even little kids can become accomplished opportunists. Recently, we caught a twelve-year-old boy who confessed to twenty-four burglaries in three months. The kid went door to door asking residents to subscribe to the local newspaper. He was so cute that many people bought a subscription from him. But the kid wasn't interested in selling papers. He was hoping that no one would answer the door. That's when he signaled to his buddies to sneak around to the backyard and enter through a milk chute or sliding glass window. Once inside, the boys grabbed everything in sight—a can of juice, crackers, jewelry, expensive radios, stereos, cameras and guns.

We finally nailed these kids when one of our officers stopped a fourteen-year-old boy who should have been in school. He was carrying a radio that we traced to one of the burglaries. When confronted with the information, the boy named two friends as accomplices. Soon after, all six boys, ages twelve to sixteen, were implicated.

The team of officers who nabbed the fourteen-year-old were part of a program called TABS, which stands for Truant Abatement Burglary Suppression. This special police unit is one of the first of its kind in the nation. We assign four off-duty cops each day to stop youths out on the streets. If the kids belong in school, they are brought to special youth centers staffed by juvenile probation officers, who contact school officials and parents. The officers have wide discretion in questioning and detaining juveniles found outside school grounds during school hours. About a third are returned to classes the same day; the rest are released to their parents.

In the two years since TABS was organized, the program has produced hundreds of success stories. One involved an officer who spotted several youngsters at a bowling alley during midday. A seventeen-year-old said he had dropped out of high school. A pat search found a .38-caliber revolver tucked inside the youth's waistband. A search of the youth's car turned up stolen coins, jewelry and a stereo set. The boy eventually admitted to pulling off a burglary that day, which was where the five $20 bills in his wallet came from.

In those parts of the city where TABS programs were introduced, burglaries decreased by 23 percent the first year. When you consider the average burglary victim in San Jose loses $1,600, that amounts to quite a savings. About 400 youths were arrested that year and 6,000 were returned to the classroom. Besides reducing the number of burglaries in San Jose, the TABS program improved school attendance figures.

NEIGHBORHOOD WATCH PROGRAMS: SIMPLE, EFFECTIVE

The Neighborhood Watch program has produced similar results. Introduced in dozens of communities across the country in recent years, the program encourages neighbors to work together to prevent crime, as did my neighbor who jotted down the license-plate number of the youths who tried to break into my house. The watch program taught him to respond to unusual happenings or suspicious characters. Members of watch programs are cautioned that if a van pulls into a nearby driveway and begins loading furniture, they should not assume their neighbors are moving. An immediate call to the neighbors or police will ensure that the movers aren't, in fact, burglars.

All a San Jose neighborhood has to do to start a watch program is to arrange a meeting with a police representative. He will come out and meet with a minimum of six neighbors and advise them on how to watch over their property, to exchange phone numbers, inform one another when they leave on vacation and report any suspicious-looking characters to police. Most of these programs are successful when neighbors use these meetings to get to know one another better. A burglar who sees Neighborhood Watch signs posted in several homes on the same block is less likely to operate in that neighborhood.

In many large urban settings, residents don't know one another. They may wave on the way to work or chat while cutting their lawns, but they probably don't know each other well enough to exchange telephone numbers. The burglar uses this to his advantage. If he knows that he can walk up to a house without anyone questioning him, he will go to work on that neighborhood. In San Jose, a burglar actually carried a stolen TV out of a house in broad daylight while a neighbor across the street was mowing his lawn.

Neighborhood Watch first came to San Jose in 1975. Since then, burglaries in those neighborhoods that have programs have decreased an average 20 percent. But San Jose is not alone. In Pleasant Valley, Maryland, a community of seventy homes in Prince George's County near Washington, D.C., a Neighborhood Watch program reduced the burglary rate from two per week to none. In the Mount Pleasant neighborhood of Providence, Rhode Island, there were fifty house burglaries a month before the state's first watch program began in 1976. Now there are only five a month. In New York, police report a nearly 20-percent dip in crime in neighborhoods with watch programs.

BURGLAR ALARMS

Organizing a watch program in your neighborhood is just one security measure you can take to protect your home. Installing a burglar alarm is another.

Whether or not you should purchase a burglar alarm system really depends on who you are, what you are afraid of and how much money you have.You should also consider whether you have young children or animals who will set off an alarm system, and whether you're absentminded, like me, and apt to set the alarm off by accident. A burglar alarm may be more of a nuisance to you than it's worth, especially if you are in little danger of a break-in to begin with.

Who Needs One?

You live on a farm where the nearest neighbor is miles down the road. While you may have expensive farm machinery and animals, you don't really have many possessions that would lure a burglar. My advice: Don't bother with an alarm. It isn't worth the expense and it wouldn't do much good, anyway.

You are a best-selling author or millionaire landowner who enjoys seclusion. Again, your neighbors live miles away. But because you are wealthy, you have lots of fine jewelry, valuable paintings and expensive antiques. My advice: You definitely need an alarm system, preferably one that is hooked into a communications system that will alert the nearest law-enforcement agency when it goes off.

You live in a large city, either in an apartment or your own house. You don't have any original Picassos on the wall, but you do fear that someone might break in while you are there, night or day. My advice: An alarm is probably a good investment to give you peace of mind.

You live in a large apartment complex that already has its own security system, including guards, locking gates and surveillance cameras. Most of the tenants in the complex work and are not at home during the daytime. My advice: Don't buy an alarm. No one is going to be around to hear it, except the burglar. Everyone knows that—especially the burglar.

You live in a suburban community with large houses that has been hit by a string of burglaries. You think the thieves may be a group of neighborhood youths, and you fear that your place may be next. My advice: Buy an alarm. Your neighbors will hear the alarm, and it may lead to the capture of the burglars.

You have a vacation home that stays empty most of the year when you're not there. The same is true of many other homes in the area. My advice: An alarm system will be useless if no one is there to react to it. It makes more sense not to keep any valuables in vacation homes. Also, you should ask any year-round residents to keep an eye on your house.

If you decide you need an alarm, spend some time learning what the different alarms can do. Contact your local police department's crime-prevention unit. Generally, the police will not recommend a specific alarm company. However, they may be willing to tell you which companies are not good, and point you toward some better ones. Also, call your local Better Business Bureau, Chamber of Commerce and any consumer protection agency. Don't rush into purchasing a system. Alarm companies are in the business of selling you their most expensive systems. One unscrupulous company promotes its alarms with advertisements that show an armed robber wearing a ski mask. As we have seen, robbery is an entirely different crime from burglary; and defending yourself from robbers has nothing to do with protection against burglars. So be wary of alarm dealers who use scare tactics to pressure you into buying an expensive system.

Basic Alarm Systems

There are two types of burglar alarms. One is the perimeter alarm. It gives a warning sound if someone attempts to enter through a window or door of your apartment or house. The other is an intrusion alarm. It gives a warning after entry has been made.

Within these two basic categories, there is a bewildering range of varieties and prices. Some systems cost a few bucks while others run well into the thousands. You must do some comparing and studying.

Most alarm systems, whether perimeter or intrusion, are activated when someone tries to enter or does enter your home. The sensor is the device that is activated to sound a warning.

Here are some of the different sensors you might choose from:

Perimeter alarms often are activated by magnetic contacts attached to doors, windows and other openings. When the door or window is opened, the magnet moves away from the switch and the alarm sounds. This is one of the most popular devices used in alarm systems.

Another sensor for perimeter alarms is the plunger contact. Plungers are concealed buttons generally used on doors. They operate like the light inside your refrigerator or auto. Open the door, and the plunger comes out and turns on the light or, in this case, activates the alarm.

One sensor used for intrusion alarms is a pressure mat. The same idea is at work when you enter a commercial shop and the sound of chimes announces your entry. When someone walks into your house, the pressure mat sets off an alarm. These types of alarms can be used in homes, but if you have small children or large pets, pressure mats are probably not for you.

Some devices project invisible infrared light beams across hallways, rooms, stairways, etc. If someone walks into that area, the beam is broken and the alarm sounds.

A passive infrared system measures heat generated within a protected space. When an individual moves into this area, his body heat is detected by a sensor that sets off the alarm.

Motion detectors have become increasingly popular among homeowners. They fill an area with ultrasound microwaves that are present in specific patterns. When someone enters and the pattern changes, the alarm system is triggered. Again, none of these three systems is the most practical for a family with children and pets.

Proximity devices are effective alarms for protecting specific objects, such as safes, file cabinets or works of art. They are useless for personal safety since the intruder must come within several inches of the object before the alarm goes off.

Panic buttons are small devices located at various spots within a home, perhaps near entrance doors and next to beds. They allow you to manually activate the alarm system if you suspect an intruder is nearby. Again, if you have children or lots of curious guests who might push these buttons, they may not be right for you.

The alarm signal itself may be a loud bell, buzzer, siren or horn. Other more expensive warning systems automatically turn on lights. More protection is offered by systems that transmit an alarm to police communications or a private security firm. Some systems are hooked up to direct-dialing telephones that, when activated, play a tape-recorded message alerting authorities of a break-in.

Which is right for you? If price is no object, you probably will go for a deluxe system that combines both perimeter and intrusion alarms hooked in to police headquarters. With some systems, private alarm companies can actually listen for movement in your house. However, these systems present potential privacy problems.

For most of us, some compromise in cost is necessary. As mentioned previously, if you have children or pets, you need to avoid alarm systems that they can easily set off. These include most of the intrusion alarms I described. Most experts will tell you that an adequate defense against the great majority of common burglars is a rather simple perimeter alarm with an audible bell or siren, combined with prominently displayed warning signs that let strangers know your house is protected.

I have even seen old unused alarm boxes fastened to outer walls with signs warning, falsely of course, that a house has an alarm. Some people recommend against these warning signs because they tip off burglars about which system is in use. I disagree. A sign will be sufficient in most cases to scare off opportunist and semipro burglars, and the highly skilled professional burglar is not going to be that worried about what system you have, because chances are he knows how to deactivate it.

For a family living in an apartment or house where some danger of burglary by opportunists exists, a fairly inexpensive perimeter alarm system with an audible bell or siren is adequate. The same is true for people who fear nighttime break-ins by violent criminals. Depending on your needs and budget, a perimeter alarm may be combined with systems that summon police or private security help, such as an intrusion alarm or panic buttons. If you have attack dogs or firearms, paying for direct communications to your police department may be an unnecessary expense. In these cases, the early warning of the perimeter alarm will give you time to wake up and take adequate defensive measures, while someone else calls police.

Extremely wealthy people, government officials or executives who run special dangers from kidnappers, terrorists or just plain kooks can expect to pay more for their peace of mind and security.

Some general reminders:

1. An alarm system is only as good as the reliability of the power supply. Good systems have emergency backup power from batteries so that a power outage or a clever burglar can't put them out of action.
2. Devices that turn the system on or off should be tamperproof.
3. In checking with police, ask about false-alarm ordinances that can cost you a bundle if your system is easily set off by accident.
4. Remember that no alarm system works unless it is turned on. Perimeter alarms should be left on at night and at all times when you are at home.

SECURITY ON A BROADER LEVEL

Many people still think if they live in a cozy suburban neighborhood they can't possibly have a crime problem. That was probably true ten years ago. But suburbia has seen such tremendous increases in crime in recent years that we're beginning to lose control.

In the inner cities, many people have long resided in apartment buildings that provide tight security. A guard who knows the tenants on a first-name basis stands at the front of the lobby and watches residents to their apartments via a television monitor. Each apartment is equipped with alarms to contact a guard in case of an emergency.

Now the demand for such elaborate security has extended to suburban communities. Many adults who once lived in stylish ranch homes are moving into townhouses and condominiums. These walled-in communities with armed guards and steel gates at the entrance provide residents with great security and peace of mind. But I don't think you need to move from a comfortable neighborhood to protect yourself from burglars.

Among other things, wherever you live you should get good insurance coverage for your possessions. Since there is no total security against burglary, you have to play the odds. One hedge against losing out is to get a solid insurance policy based on the replacement value of your possessions, not the purchase value. Many people who have paid their homeowner or rental insurance faithfully for years are sent into a state of shock when they learn their policy covered only 20 percent of the replacement value of jewelry and furs.

Keep a personal inventory and make sure everything is marked for identification purposes. Most police departments have tools available for residents to engrave their names and social security numbers on TV sets, stereos and other valuables.

In recent years, the police have gotten much better at recovering stolen property. As mentioned previously, most major police departments conduct sting operations that take in millions of dollars' worth of property each year. But we have no way of knowing who owns the stuff if it's not properly marked for identification.

Here are some pointers that you should review with your family to see that your home is secure. Then take the test on pages 147–149 to see how far you have to go.

1. When you are away, make your house or apartment look as if someone is there. All burglars want to hit an empty house. For five bucks you can purchase an electronic timer to control lights, radio and TV to make your place

look lived in. The secret is to simulate your pattern of living using these electronic controls and not to exaggerate it for the burglar's sake. Many homeowners leave their radio blaring so someone outside will hear. That doesn't make sense unless you generally listen to music that loud. Instead, tune the radio to an all-talk show and keep the sound at a normal conversational level.

2. Lock all doors and windows. This may seem obvious, but more than half of all burglaries occur because someone left a door or window open. Also, don't leave your house unlocked even if you're just going to drop the kids off at school. A burglary takes only a couple of minutes.

3. When you're on vacation have someone pick up all handbills, newspapers and the mail. Nothing is more inviting to a burglar than a mailbox stuffed with letters postmarked several days earlier or a porch full of week-old newspapers. You might as well put an open-house sign in your front yard. It's better to ask neighbors to pick up mail and papers so you don't take a chance with the mail carrier or paperboy ripping you off. While you're at it, ask your neighbor or pay someone to mow the lawn and move your cars around in the driveway. If it's a neighbor, promise them you'll do the same when they go on vacation.

4. Think about getting a house-sitter. Perhaps a relative or friend, or even a neighbor's kid you trust. It's well worth a nominal fee. After all, the rich usually have servants watch their property when they're gone. Or they hire someone for that purpose. I've known several police officers and their wives who stayed in luxurious mansions and apartments for a couple of weeks for the vacationing owners.

5. Check the quality of your doors and window locks. Ask your local police department or crime-prevention bureau for help. You should have a dead-bolt lock on all doors, and secondary locks on sliding doors and windows. As

chairman of the crime-prevention subcommittee for the International Association of Chiefs of Police, I know that many police departments have active crime-prevention bureaus that offer free inspection and advice. It is a service you ought to ask for.

6. Take an inventory of all your household goods, and record serial numbers. Borrow an electric engraving pen from your library or police department and put your driver's license or social security number on appliances, stereos, televisions, home computers and any other large items. For those articles that cannot be engraved—china, silverware, jewelry, etc.—photograph them next to an index card with your name and address.

7. Make sure the outside of your home is well lit, particularly the entrances. Check your house to see if tall shrubs permit a burglar to shield his activities from suspicious neighbors.

8. Make sure everyone in your family, including children, is aware of the security precautions you have taken. It doesn't do much good to have sophisticated locks and alarm systems if someone forgets to lock a side gate.

9. Get to know your neighbors. If you can get ten or more people together, most police departments will send an expert to help start a Neighborhood Watch program.

10. Don't hide keys around the house. Many burglars watch kids get a house key from a flowerpot or some other hiding place to unlock the door, then wait until no one is around to take advantage of their discovery of your secret spot.

11. Don't open your door for strangers. If someone you don't know can't provide credentials, tell him to come back when someone else is home.

12. Leave shades and blinds partly open when you are away. Many people make the mistake of closing everything up. That makes it obvious to even the casual observer that no one is home.

13. When you go out, don't leave notes in plain sight saying when you'll return home. You're telling a burglar when to raid your house.

14. Don't tell others about your valuable possessions. A homeowner who lets his neighbors know that anyone caught entering his house will get their head blown off with his shotgun is inviting someone to steal that gun. You increase your chances of being burglarized if you spread word about your valuables.

15. Vary your routine. If you water the garden, go grocery shopping and walk the dog at the same time each week, the burglar will hit your house shortly after you leave.

16. Do not list your phone number in city directories. Some burglars call in advance to make sure no one is home. If a burglar can't find your number in the book, he may decide against breaking in. If you must have your number published, use an answering machine to make callers think you might be home.

17. If you like pets, think about getting a watchdog. It may not be the answer to all your security woes, but at least a dog can alert your neighbors that someone is lurking nearby.

18. Don't ever give your ring of keys to a stranger, such as a parking attendant. Instead, take off the car key and keep the rest in your pocket. If you must give your keys to a cleaning person or friend, make sure he or she can be trusted.

19. Don't store large amounts of cash, jewelry or other small valuables in your house. Keep them in a safe-deposit box.

20. Be careful how you safeguard your house. Some people have used measures so extreme they ended up paying for it with their lives. One family put steel bars outside their windows. Not only did the bars keep burglars out, but they trapped family members inside when their house caught fire.

While your really valuable belongings should be kept in a locked safe or safe-deposit box, there are some alternative hiding places within a house or apartment to keep other, less expensive items away from burglars.

1. Inside the bases of lamps or telephones.
2. Inside a phony heating or air-conditioning duct.
3. In a cabinet or other storage area concealed from casual view.
4. Inside a fake electrical wall socket. These are available at many stores.
5. Inside appliances such as washers and dryers, pool filters and even old TV sets.

Don't hesitate to use your own ingenuity to come up with other hiding places. One person I know puts his cash and jewelry inside a hollow turkey in his freezer. A word of caution: Don't forget where you have stashed something, and make sure that your heirs know about whatever it is you've hidden away, in the event something unexpectedly happens to you.

HOME SECURITY CHECKLIST TEST

The following is a test to see how burglarproof your residence is. You should be able to answer yes to all thirty-four questions before you consider your house or apartment secure.

Doors

1. Does front door have a peephole?
2. Can you lock your doors from the inside with a key?
3. Are entrance doors solid?
4. Do they have dead-bolt locks with a minimum 1-inch throw?

5. If hinge pins are outside, are they nonremovable?
6. Does door fit against doorjamb securely?
7. Is doorjamb tightly fastened?
8. Is strike plate tightly fastened to doorjamb?
9. Were locks changed when you moved in?

Windows

10. Have double-hung windows been drilled so that the top and bottom sashes can be secured with bolts?
11. Do metal or basement windows have auxiliary locks?
12. Can windows left open for ventilation be secured?
13. Do curtains or drapes fully cover windows?
14. Is window air conditioner secured from inside?

Garage

15. Does door close tightly?
16. Does overhead door have a track padlock?
17. Do you keep overhead door closed and locked when not in use?
18. Do you remove vehicle keys even when garage is locked?
19. Can garage light be turned on from inside house?

Outside

20. Are shrubs and tree limbs cut below window level?
21. Is residence number visible from street?
22. Are front and back entrances well lit?
23. Are bicycles, mowers, ladders, etc., kept inside?
24. Have you engraved identifying numbers on your prop-

erty and put Neighborhood Watch program stickers in your windows?

Vacations

25. Do you stop deliveries?
26. Do you notify police and neighbors?
27. Do you set light timers?
28. Is your yard taken care of?
29. Do you arrange for handbills to be picked up?

Crime Checks

30. Do you keep most of your cash in the bank?
31. Do you keep a list of all valuable property, credit cards and serial numbers?
32. Have you and your children memorized the police telephone emergency number?
33. Do you avoid displaying valuables to strangers?
34. If you have a gun, is it kept in a safe place?

A NOTE ON CARS

Most people don't worry much about auto theft in comparison with their concern for their household goods. Until recently, a majority of auto thieves were teenagers pulling a prank, or a stranded motorist who didn't feel like waiting for a bus and decided to help himself to transportation.

But there's been a major change in automobile theft—one that ought to have you deeply concerned about the safety of your car. Ten years ago, 80 percent of all stolen vehicles were recovered within a block or two of the original location. Today, more than 1 million vehicles are stolen every year by hardened professionals who can take a car in less than a minute with tools that cost less than forty bucks.

Why has the sophisticated criminal turned his attention to auto theft? Two reasons. Auto theft is extremely low-risk today. It is viewed as a victimless, nonviolent crime. In the unlikely event that an auto thief gets caught, chances are that he will never spend a day behind bars, because what little room is left in crowded prisons is reserved for rapists and killers. The other reason is that there is a high demand for used cars. Many stolen cars end up in chop shops, where the parts are salvaged for resale. Because the new-car market is down and people are keeping their cars longer, criminals have seen the demand for used parts soar. As a result, the recovery rate of stolen cars has now dropped to 55 percent.

So, given the current prevalence of auto theft, what can you do to protect your car from thieves? Try the following tips:

1. First and most obvious, insure your car. Without adequate vehicle insurance, you will simply have nowhere to turn if your car is stolen.
2. Always lock your car. It's amazing how often a chagrined motorist will tell a police officer that he left his car unlocked because he was only going to be gone a minute.
3. Keep items such as CB radios and tape decks hidden when you leave your car.
4. If you have spent extra money for nice wheels on your cars, spend a few more bucks for special wheel locks. Most burglars know that chrome wheels are among the hottest items in demand.
5. Park in busy, well-lit areas where others will be likely to see a burglar trying to steal your car.
6. Whenever you leave your car, carry the vehicle registration with you. If your car is stolen, reporting the license-plate number won't do much good if the thief has changed

plates. The registration number will assist the police in tracking down your vehicle.

7. Cars with open hatchback windows, and station wagons, allow burglars a free inspection of the contents inside. If you own this type of car, use a large piece of canvas or a blanket to cover any valuables you may be carrying.

10
CON ARTISTS AND THEIR GAMES

My first burglary call as a rookie cop in Harlem taught me a valuable lesson—anyone can become a victim of con games.

The year was 1956. A woman had called police to report that a man was trying to break into her apartment. My partner and I responded Code 3—that is, with red lights and siren. When we arrived, I eagerly ran up the stairs to the fourth-floor landing where we were told a man was trying to force open an apartment door. My more experienced partner walked calmly behind me. To my astonishment, a white man dressed in a sailor's uniform was standing in the doorway in this all-black neighborhood.

After some questioning, we determined that the sailor wasn't a prowler or burglar at all. He was the victim of a trick called the Murphy game. The sailor, who was visiting New York for the first time, had been taken by one of the many sophisticated con artists infesting Times Square who specialize in selecting young, gullible targets on the lookout for female companionship.

In the case of the sailor, the con man had lured him by describing an apartment in Harlem that was home to a prostitution ring. Then he skillfully haggled just enough with the sailor over the price to make a convincing sales pitch. As the two of them rode the uptown subway, the con man reminded the sailor how lucky he was to have a guide because the area was so dangerous. At least the con man was right on that score.

As they approached the apartment, the con man stopped his client with one last warning. He said, as delightful as the girls were inside the apartment, they provided sex for money and might steal the sailor's wallet and other personal belongings. The girls, he whispered, have been known to raid a man's pockets while he was in a compromising position. So the helpful con man pulled an official-looking manila envelope from his jacket and instructed the sailor to place his valuables inside. The sailor, being no fool, insisted upon an itemized receipt for his valuables. The con man consented and drew up a list.

Since the sailor was not known to the people inside the apartment, the con man said he would go ahead by a minute or so to assure the prostitutes that the sailor was not an undercover policeman. The sailor waited for a moment, then approached the apartment as instructed and knocked on the door. Instead of arriving at a house of prostitution, the sailor had frightened an entire family by pounding on their door in the middle of the night.

The con man, of course, had not gone near the apartment. Instead, he continued up the stairs to the roof and ran to a connecting apartment house.

I tried to explain to the poor sailor that he had been taken, but he didn't hear me. He kept waving a piece of paper in my face and saying over and over, "But he gave me a receipt." After making out the crime report and sending the sailor on his way, my partner told me that the victim was luckier than most victims of the Murphy game. At least he had enough money left for a cab to drive him back to his ship. In this case, the con man had thoughtfully left four bucks under the pretense that the sailor might want to tip a prostitute who was especially accommodating.

Upon resuming our patrol that night, I remarked to my partner that I just couldn't believe that someone could be so dumb that he would turn over his valuables to a perfect stranger. My partner laughed and said, "You'll see a lot of things that you won't believe in the next few years." He was right. Some of the most successful and wealthiest people in the world fall for con games. Even people who should know better, such as police officers, are taken.

My partner told me that one of the very same cops who

responded on the prowler run had fallen for a con game a couple of years earlier during a routine patrol on a Sunday morning. The cop had been approached by a respectable-looking man who politely inquired about where he could cash a government pension check. The cop told him, No chance. Back then, everything was closed on Sundays. The man shrugged his shoulders, lowered his head in despair and told the officer a classic sob story. He simply had to get to Arkansas that night because of a death in his family. The man said he was so desperate that he was willing to take half of the actual value of the check just so he could make the trip. The man went on to say that it was his mother who'd died suddenly and that he could not wait until Monday to cash his check. The funeral was scheduled for the first thing tomorrow morning.

I listened unbelievingly as my veteran patrol partner chuckled. The officer actually bought the story. He figured that no one would ever try to con a cop. When the officer asked about the amount of the check, the con man knew he had his mark hooked. The cop actually bargained with the man on the amount and settled on keeping 60 percent. But before he handed over the money, the officer insisted on a clear endorsement and two pieces of identification from the con man. He wanted to be protected just in case anything went wrong.

Of course, the ending of this story resembles that of the sailor who kept saying "But he gave me a receipt." Instead, the cop who had been conned out of $50 kept saying, "But it was a government check and he had identification." The check, along with the identification, however, had been stolen from the true owner.

The moral of these two stories is that we are all potential victims of con games. Con men (and women) see themselves as the kings (and queens) of the criminal class. They look down on thugs, who resort to physical force and weapons to commit crimes. Con artists rely on their wits. They feel they are superior because they can achieve the same profitable results without violence.

To their victims, con men usually appear honest and trust-

155

worthy. And persuasive. They try to make the victim think he is getting a great deal. Often, they also like to impress their prospective victims with a show of wealth, with meetings in luxury hotels, in airplanes or foreign countries. Some cons aren't faking when they show off their belongings. Police routinely arrest wealthy entrepreneurs who collected much of their fortunes operating fraudulent schemes.

Recently, a San Jose area executive was arrested on suspicion of bilking more than $5 million from thousands of members of his discount-buying service. The executive advertised a $495 membership fee that entitled members to discounts up to 60 percent off the price of various goods and services. When one dissatisfied customer complained that the $1,345 in furniture he ordered was never received, the executive pulled a .38-caliber gun from his boot and threatened the man.

Like the executive, most con artists are good actors who fool their victims with the nice-guy approach. They are shrewd psychologists who have mastered the art of making themselves appear legitimate. While most con artists are amoral, they are not violent. They operate on the premise that their victims deserve their fate.

Con artists are usually most successful when they seek out victims who are lonely, willing to help others and have a sense of charity. Ultimately, the con will exploit his victims' assets, and often he'll do it with their willing cooperation.

Elderly women who live alone are the most frequent targets. But con men enjoy pulling off the most audacious scams and duping so-called bright and successful people.

If you think you are immune to their antics, consider a recent case in which an elderly couple was charged with attempting to bilk President Reagan and his wife, Nancy, in a fraudulent deal to buy the Reagans' Pacific Palisades home.

A seventy-four-year-old grandmother and her sixty-year-old husband tried to pass themselves off as millionaire home buyers. They actually had succeeded in getting an escrow claim and used the deed to con other people into giving them money by pretending to have the inside track on the Reagan house

Prosecutors in the case charged that the con artists were so persuasive that Mrs. Reagan had the swimming pool drained so they could inspect it.

In all, the pair obtained $123,000 from people who thought they were dealing with a couple who invested millions in houses similar to those owned by the President. One of the victims was the couple's own real estate agent. The Reagans apparently had listed the house at $1.9 million and the realtor agreed to arrange a $1 million loan during escrow until the couple could come up with the money supposedly due them from an inheritance. Of course, the elderly couple had no such wealthy connections. They were actually living on a disability pension. Yet by dressing fancy, acting rich and telling a few lies, they nearly got away with duping the President of the United States.

There are nearly as many con games as there are con artists. While I will list some of the more common schemes, bear in mind that con artists are always thinking up new variations.

BANK EXAMINER

The con man identifies himself as a police officer and enlists the help of his victim to trap an employee who is embezzling money from a bank. The con artist persuades the victim to help authorities test the honesty of the bank employee by withdrawing substantial funds. When the money is handed over to the con artist for examination, he issues the victim a phony but official-looking receipt and disappears.

A seventy-seven-year-old San Jose woman, Katherine Eifert, lost $1,800 from her savings account and thousands more in stock certificates in a bank-examiner scam. She received a telephone call one morning from a woman who identified herself as a San Jose police lieutenant. The caller told Mrs. Eifert that police suspected money was being taken from her account by bank employees and said a detective would drop by her house. Five minutes later, a man dressed in a suit and tie showed up on her doorstep, flashing a gold police badge. He asked Mrs.

Eifert if she would look at some photographs of suspects. Then the con man told Mrs. Eifert that in order for police to arrest the suspects she would have to withdraw all her funds from the bank. The phony officer escorted the woman to her branch, where she made the withdrawal and handed over the money and certificates. The officer thanked the woman for her cooperation, complimented her on fulfilling her civic duty and said he would get back to her in a couple of days.

The next time Mrs. Eifert talked with police, she was reporting the theft. To this day, she hasn't recovered her money.

THE GOLD MINE

Some of the most successful con games are remodeled old schemes. Back in the frontier days, when gold mines yielded great fortunes, con men sold discounted shares in petered-out mines to the most prominent people in town. This was done by salting the mines with enough real nuggets and then arranging for a prominent local official to "discover" the gold. As expected, people rushed to get in on the latest bonanza. Today, this scam may be worked with shares in a new computer company, but there are still bogus gold mines awaiting the unwary.

In northern California, two partners bilked 800 investors out of an estimated $11 million in an Alaskan gold-mining scam. The two men pleaded guilty to nine counts of securities violations in connection with the scheme, which promised investors fantastic returns. The investors all believed the promises and fancy brochures. Not one chose to inspect the phony gold mines in Alaska. While some victims initially received handsome dividends (a typical ploy to enlist more investors), most lost everything they invested. The victims ranged from an IBM employee ($160,000) to a former army first sergeant ($65,000) to an eighty-seven-year-old man who lost his entire savings and was forced to refinance his home.

Such fraudulent investment schemes have become extremely

popular in recent years because so many people are looking for tax shelters and hedges against inflation. This is particularly true in real estate, where extraordinary profits reaped in the Sunbelt states in the past ten years have encouraged others to blindly put their money in crooked deals.

PIGEON DROP

Like most schemes, this one sounds ridiculous, but believe me it occurs every day. The con artist will usually select his victim outside a bank where he has seen the person deposit money—the obvious sign that there is money available to steal. The con artist will initially try to win the confidence of the victim by approaching him and voicing suspicion of a third party, who in reality is the con man's partner. The con will tell the stranger that he can get his hands on a quick ten grand if he puts up $1,000 in cash. He'll make up some story, for example, he and his buddy found the money and did not turn it in to the government. Or they are drug dealers who need the cash quickly to make a big score on a new shipment. They need money as a down payment to give to a lawyer, who is holding the find, or a pusher, who has the drugs, before they get the loot. The trouble, the con artist says, is that he only has $200. If the victim will lend him another $800, he'll split his share of the ten grand with him. The con artist, who is much more skilled than I am at making this all sound believable, tells the victim that he doesn't want this third party to get all the cash for himself.

The game works because the con artist is successful at whetting the appetite of a stranger eager to make a quick killing. In this case, who would pass up the opportunity to make $5,000 in exchange for a down payment of $800? When you're talking that kind of profit, tax free at that, many people don't care where it comes from. There are enough reports in the media of people finding large sums of money or making millions from drug sales to make the scam credible.

When the victim agrees to go along, lending the con man

$800, he is then left holding the bag when both con artists never return.

JAMAICAN SWITCH

This con game is fairly straightforward. But again it is hard to believe that it is successful so frequently. A man with a foreign accent presents himself as a stranger to America, with a large sum of money that he fears will be stolen. The victim, who is coming out of a bank or sitting on a park bench when the con man approaches, will often suggest that the man deposit the money in a bank. But the con artist claims to be fearful of banks and asks the victim to take him to his bank. Once they get to the victim's branch, the con man says he is still uneasy and asks the victim to withdraw a large sum to prove that you can get your money back anytime you want. If the con man played his cards right, the victim has begun to feel sorry for this rather helpless newcomer and agrees to help him out. After the withdrawal is made, the con artist remains doubtful and suggests that he combine his cash with the victim's in the same account. The victim sees an opportunity to perhaps make some money himself by duping the naive foreigner.

In the process of redepositing the money the victim took out of his account, the con man switches the package of money with an identical one filled with shredded newspaper. As the victim tries to deposit the money, the con artist leaves the bank with the loot.

THE WILLIAMSON GANG

American consumers have been bilked out of millions of dollars a year by this group of home-repair fraud artists. They operate their business knowing that law-enforcement officers have been unable to end their tradition of rip-offs for six decades. Chances are they never will be stopped. Some of their schemes have included the sale of cheap, machine-made products misrepresented as Oriental rugs and fine woolens, as well as fancy barn paint that washes off after the first rain.

Named after a family that specialized in bilking homeowners across the country, the Williamson Gang now consists of more than 300 adult "family" members and associates, according to the California Department of Justice. The contemporary gang specializes in fraudulent household repairs. The members often make outlandish verbal guarantees—for instance, that a product will seal all leaks. In reality, members dilute products with crankcase oil and aluminum paint to make them go further.

The Williamson Gang has been known to smuggle pieces of termite-infested wood into homes to convince potential victims that their residences need extensive work. Another ploy is to offer extremely low rates for tree-pruning services and then afterward inform the homeowner that the price quoted was per branch, not per tree.

How does the Williamson Gang get away with these practices? By working neighborhoods where residents are likely to be elderly, using young boys to make convincing sales pitches on behalf of their "daddy," and impressing prospective victims with new trucks and fancy equipment.

Many victims are reluctant to admit they have been duped. Often, they do not know they have been swindled until after the offense has taken place. In some cases, they never realize it at all.

By following these tips, you can protect yourself against Williamson Gang members or their kind in your state.

1. Never let a stranger talk you into believing your home needs repair. If in doubt, ask a professional.
2. If someone comes to your door, don't purchase their services without checking for proper identification, building contractor's licenses and city or county permits. Then call the Better Business Bureau to make sure the company is legitimate and does honest work.
3. Always demand a written estimate. When the job is done,

don't accept excuses that purport to explain a significant jump in cost. Pay by check or credit card. Never pay in cash.

4. Don't be deceived by a low price. The reason most people get tricked by the Williamson Gang is that they can't pass up a steal. In the end, however, they are the ones who are taken. Remember, you get what you pay for.

CHARITIES

A thin, clean-shaven man clad in modest clothing knocks on your door. He says he is a volunteer for a charity and asks for a few minutes of your time. He starts to talk about the men and women left to rot in prison who have been abandoned by their families. With all that time on their hands, he says, wouldn't it be nice if they had a Bible to read? Well, his organization wants to distribute a Bible to every prisoner in your state. For only $25, five prisoners can gain inspiration from the scriptures.

Sounds like a worthy goal. Only there is no intention to purchase any Bibles. The phony Bible company puts the donations to work this way: 60 percent to the solicitor, 20 percent to his manager and 20 percent to the operator of the scam.

A teenager appears on your doorstep with a fifty-cent candy bar. His name is Joey and he wants to sell you candy to raise money for a youth center to keep kids like him off the streets. Most adults find it difficult to turn down an innocent-looking youth.

However, there are no plans to build a youth center. After Joey has sold his candy bars, he hands the money to an adult waiting around the corner in a car. So do four other youngsters who covered other neighborhoods. The kids get a small hourly wage for their efforts. The adult pockets the rest. For years, police departments have received reports of the use of children to peddle overpriced goods and misuse the names of legitimate charitable organizations to collect contributions.

I don't want to discourage you from making charitable contributions. Nor do I want you to think that all solicitors for charitable organizations are phonies. However, enough fraudulent collectors are making the rounds in neighborhoods across the country that you need to make sure that your money is being spent the way you intended.

Many states have a charitable solicitation law that requires people going door to door to carry a brochure that has the name and address of the charity, the percentage of donations that will be used as direct fund-raising expenses, and whether the organization qualifies as a charitable tax exemption, so you can take a legitimate tax deduction on your contribution. You should demand such information before ever contributing money to strangers.

Some other tips:

1. Ask the solicitor for an envelope to mail a check to the organization. Then review the charity with the Better Business Bureau or local consumer affairs agency.
2. Never make out a check to an individual. Always use the charity's name.
3. Organizations such as the Red Cross or Boy Scouts value their reputations so much that they welcome scrutiny. Chances are that solicitors representing these charities are legitimate. However, if you are in doubt, call the organization directly to confirm that they are raising funds in your neighborhood.

MAIL FRAUD

"Now you can earn extra money in your spare time by doing simple, pleasant work addressing envelopes in your own home. No experience needed. No boss looking over your shoulder. You can even work while watching television. We'll pay you thirty cents an envelope. Submit 300 envelopes, and we'll send you $90. We guarantee it. A one-time registration fee of $15 will be returned after you address 200 envelopes. Please rush check or money order to . . ."

After seeing this advertisement, 50,000 persons sent checks to a dozen "work-at-home" firms. The applicants, who included nurses, teachers and housewives, wanted to supplement their incomes by working at home. Many were ambitious college graduates in their early thirties; others were retirees living on fixed incomes. Over a three-year period, they paid more than $650,000 in registration fees.

Most of the people never received envelopes, nor were their fees ever refunded. Like most victims, many were too embarrassed to report the rip-offs to police. A two-year investigation by the U.S. Postal Service led to a federal indictment charging four California men with thirty-four counts of mail fraud. The indictment marked the first time that a postal-service investigation into envelope-stuffing schemes ended in criminal charges. Most of the time, the cons get off free.

The list of fraudulent offers is really endless. Computer dating. Dance lessons. Freezer plans. Fortune tellers. Health clubs. Job placement. Medical quackery. Talent scouts. Pyramid schemes. All lure their share of cons waiting to take advantage of anyone who has an extra dollar to spend.

Here are some general rules to follow:

1. Don't rush. If someone says the bargain is a one-day-only special, chances are he doesn't want you to investigate his background. If the "bargain" involves a substantial investment, take your time and consult a lawyer or accountant.

2. Don't be fooled by appearances. Remember the elderly couple who collected money on the premise they were dealing with the Reagans.

3. Don't give cash to strangers. Use another form of payment that allows you to cancel payment afterward or at least keep a record of the transaction.

4. Don't be too embarrassed to report that you've been swindled. It's the only shot you'll have at recovering your

funds and it allows the police the chance to catch the con artists.

5. To help stop this kind of crime, testify in court against the swindlers. Con men rarely stop pulling off scams after an arrest. About the only thing that will stop them is conviction and a stiff jail term.

Protecting yourself from con artists, in other words, requires healthy skepticism, reasonable alertness, and common sense; the qualities I have suggested throughout this book that will bring you safety from any number of potential criminals.

If this book serves you well, it will leave you—beyond all of the tips and strategies and specific pieces of advice—with a much clearer vision and perspective on crime than you had. It will hone your good instincts and allow you to use them more wisely. Your greater awareness, your sharper sensibility will permit you, I believe, to live safe and sane.

Appendix A
CRIME COMPARISONS

Here are some crime comparisons of major cities in the United States for 1982, which I've compiled from FBI reports and census information.

MURDER (PER 100,000 POP.)

1. Miami 53
2. St. Louis 50
3. Newark 48
4. Detroit 43
5. Houston 42
6. New Orleans 41
7. Atlanta 35
8. Cleveland 34
9. Dallas 33
10. Birmingham 32
11. Washington, D.C. 30
12. Baltimore 28
    Los Angeles 28
13. Oakland 27
14. Fort Worth 26
15. New York 24
16. San Antonio 23
17. Chicago 22
    Las Vegas 22
18. Kansas City 21
    Oklahoma City 21
    Tampa 21

19. Long Beach 19
    Memphis 19
    Philadelphia 19
20. Boston 17
21. Austin 16
    Columbus 16
    San Francisco 16
22. Indianapolis 15
    Nashville 15
    Sacramento 15
23. Cincinnati 14
    Denver 14
    Jacksonville 14
24. Louisville 12
    Phoenix 12
    Pittsburgh 12
    Rochester 12
25. Wichita 11
26. Milwaukee 10
    Minneapolis 10
    Portland 10
27. El Paso 9

Tucson 9
28. Albuquerque 8
    San Diego 8
    Tulsa 8
29. Omaha 6

San Jose 6
Seattle 6
Virginia Beach 6
30. St. Paul 3

FORCIBLE RAPE (PER 100,000 POP.)

1. Newark 179
2. Miami 150
3. Tampa 144
4. Atlanta 136
5. Oakland 127
6. Dallas 118
7. Fort Worth 117
8. Cleveland 109
   Memphis 109
9. Portland 106
10. Denver 103
11. Detroit 98
12. Kansas City 95
13. Oklahoma City 93
14. Los Angeles 90
15. Seattle 86
16. New Orleans 85
    San Francisco 85
17. Indianapolis 84
    Minneapolis 84
18. Birmingham 80
    St. Paul 80
19. Long Beach 76
20. Cincinnati 75
21. Jacksonville 73
22. Las Vegas 70
    Columbus 70

Nashville 70
St. Louis 70
23. Baltimore 69
    Tucson 69
24. Wichita 68
25. Sacramento 67
    San Jose 67
26. Austin 66
    Boston 66
    Washington, D.C. 66
27. Toledo 65
28. Tulsa 62
29. Albuquerque 58
30. Pittsburgh 55
31. Omaha 54
    Phoenix 54
32. Philadelphia 50
    Rochester 50
    New York 50
33. El Paso 49
    San Antonio 49
34. San Diego 48
35. Chicago 37
36. Louisville 36
    Virginia Beach 36
37. Milwaukee 30

ROBBERY (PER 100,000 POP.)

1. Newark 2343
2. Miami 1439
3. Washington, D.C. 1436
4. New York 1357
5. Detroit 1344
6. Boston 1174
7. Baltimore 1172
8. St. Louis 1079
9. San Francisco 1033
10. Atlanta 978
11. Cleveland 924
12. Oakland 918
13. Pittsburgh 903
14. Los Angeles 900
15. New Orleans 894
16. Long Beach 786
17. Houston 775
18. Portland 760
19. Minneapolis 694
20. Las Vegas 675
21. Memphis 673
22. Tampa 646
23. Philadelphia 629
24. Kansas City 612
25. Dallas 607
26. Columbus 597
27. Louisville 567
28. Fort Worth 561
29. Sacramento 549
30. Seattle 511
31. Toledo 502
32. Denver 475
33. Rochester 474
34. Birmingham 451
35. Oklahoma City 435
36. Indianapolis 432
37. Cincinnati 415
38. Jacksonville 374
39. Nashville 363
40. San Diego 349
41. Milwaukee 326
42. St. Paul 313
43. Phoenix 302
44. Tulsa 286
45. San Antonio 268
46. Tucson 267
47. San Jose 264
48. Wichita 240
49. Omaha 230
50. El Paso 210
51. Honolulu 184
52. Austin 177

BURGLARIES (PER 100,000 POP.)

1. Tampa 3933
2. Detroit 3909
3. St. Louis 3777
4. Portland 3720
5. Dallas 3556
6. Atlanta 3479
7. Fort Worth 3373
8. Las Vegas 3316
9. Sacramento 3285
10. Denver 3246
11. Kansas City 3191
12. Columbus 3117
13. Miami 3092
14. St. Paul 3089
15. Minneapolis 3082
16. Oklahoma City 3063

17. Newark 2999
18. Boston 2969
19. Cleveland 2924
20. Rochester 2899
21. Birmingham 2893
22. Toledo 2805
23. Oakland 2780
24. Phoenix 2745
25. Seattle 2639
26. Memphis 2583
27. Austin 2457
28. New York 2444
29. San Antonio 2443
30. Louisville 2414
31. Long Beach 2342
32. Washington, D.C. 2322
33. Cincinnati 2263
34. Jacksonville 2231

35. Albuquerque 2226
36. New Orleans 2158
37. Indianapolis 2153
38. Wichita 2145
39. Nashville 2080
40. Baltimore 2047
41. San Francisco 1980
42. San Jose 1955
43. Pittsburgh 1904
44. San Diego 1801
45. El Paso 1679
46. Omaha 1662
47. Milwaukee 1589
48. Philadelphia 1372
49. Virginia Beach 1194
50. Chicago 1074
51. Tucson 641

AGGRAVATED ASSAULT (PER 100,000 POP.)

1. Miami 1208
2. Tampa 1201
3. Newark 1139
4. St. Louis 1019
5. Portland 879
6. San Francisco 832
7. Oakland 828
8. Atlanta 823
   Baltimore 823
9. Kansas City 778
10. Boston 716
11. Los Angeles 672
12. Dallas 635
13. Rochester 626
14. El Paso 618
15. New York 605
16. Washington, D.C. 573
17. Cleveland 570

18. Fort Worth 526
19. Jacksonville 519
20. Tucson 514
21. Detroit 506
22. New Orleans 486
23. Oklahoma City 485
24. Cincinnati 479
25. Seattle 474
26. Omaha 469
27. Albuquerque 449
28. Birmingham 445
29. Sacramento 430
30. Indianapolis 410
31. Phoenix 395
32. Dallas 390
33. San Antonio 380
   Tulsa 380
34. Memphis 362

35. St. Paul 361
36. Minneapolis 353
37. Long Beach 348
38. Philadelphia 340
39. Las Vegas 334
40. Pittsburgh 297
41. Wichita 280
42. Chicago 276
43. Nashville 262

44. Columbus 253
45. San Diego 244
46. Louisville 241
47. San Jose 225
48. Houston 216
49. Milwaukee 195
50. Toledo 185
51. Austin 170
52. Virginia Beach 104

Appendix B
POLICE FORCE COMPARISONS

POLICE (PER 100,000 POP.)*

1. Cleveland 348		25. Denver 196	
2. New York 337		26. St. Paul 195	
3. Milwaukee 316		27. Minneapolis 193	
4. Chicago 313		28. Atlanta 190	
5. Newark 300		29. Phoenix 188	
6. Boston 287		30. Columbus 187	
7. Cincinnati 266		31. Tulsa 183	
8. Miami 266		32. Houston 182	
9. Philadelphia 258		33. Dallas 177	
10. San Francisco 257		34. Fort Worth 175	
11. Baltimore 250		35. Oakland 173	
12. Oklahoma City 250		36. Jacksonville 170	
13. Washington, D.C. 244		37. Tucson 168	
14. Sacramento 244		38. Albuquerque 166	
15. Birmingham 228		39. Pittsburgh 166	
16. Nashville 227		40. Louisville 165	
17. Las Vegas 226		41. Austin 162	
18. Los Angeles 226		42. Long Beach 160	
19. St. Louis 220		43. Omaha 155	
20. New Orleans 216		44. Tampa 154	
21. Detroit 208		45. Wichita 153	
22. Indianapolis 203		46. Rochester 152	
23. Memphis 200		47. San Antonio 151	
24. Kansas City 198		48. Toledo 151	

*From 1981 FBI Crime in the United States
Latest published statistics.